Ballyhoo!

POSTERS AS PORTRAITURE

Ballyhoo!

POSTERS AS PORTRAITURE

WENDY WICK REAVES

NATIONAL PORTRAIT GALLERY | SMITHSONIAN

Published to accompany an exhibition at the
National Portrait Gallery, Smithsonian Institution

May 8, 2008–February 8, 2009

© 2008 Smithsonian Institution

ISBN: 978-0-295-98862-7
Library of Congress Control Number: 2008925960

Photography: Mark Gulezian, National Portrait Gallery

Editorial and production management: Dru Dowdy,
Head of Publications, National Portrait Gallery

Designer: Nancy Bratton,
Nancy Bratton Design, Washington, D.C.

Printer: Engelhardt und Bauer, Karlsruhe, Germany

Distributed by the University of Washington Press
P.O. Box 50096
Seattle, WA 98145-5096
www.washington.edu/uwpress

Printed in Germany

Front cover: Bette Midler by Richard Amsel, color
photolithographic poster, 1973. National Portrait
Gallery, Smithsonian Institution; gift of Jack Rennert.
Reproduced in full on page 130.

*Frontispiece: Blixtens Broder (Brother of the
Lightning).* William S. Hart by Gunnar Håkansson, color
lithographic poster, 1922. National Portrait Gallery,
Smithsonian Institution

Back cover: Poster Calendar 1896 by Edward Penfield,
color lithograph, 1896. National Portrait Gallery,
Smithsonian Institution

Contents

John Gilbert and Lillian Gish in ~~

La Bohéme

FROM THE FAMOUS PUCCINI OPERA

Ballyhoo!: Posters as Portraiture
Wendy Wick Reaves

What could be less subtle than the pictorial poster, blaring out its message with large scale, loud colors, and bold graphics? Yet, as print historian A. Hyatt Mayor once pointed out, posters competing in a busy visual environment are "pictures meant to be seen by people who did not mean to see them." The audience may, by implication, be absorbing the persuasive message on an inattentive, or even subconscious, level. We are used to decoding the poster as advertising or propaganda, intuitively understanding how the intersection of words and image informs us. But what if we consider the poster as a form of popular portraiture? How does the presence of a recognizable figure, in conjunction with those other elements, operate on our consciousness?

The National Portrait Gallery's poster collection offers some insight into how a famous face can enhance the message of posted advertising and, conversely, how posters have defined and disseminated images of prominent American figures. The triple histories of poster aesthetics, celebrity promotion, and advertising are interwoven, and each strand informs the others. Furthermore, since posters draw so heavily from the popular culture, we can catch a glimpse into each generation's attitudes toward people. What are the prevailing standards at that moment for masculinity, ideals of beauty, acceptable levels of nudity, sexual boundaries, or racial diversity? Posters, which aim for mainstream accessibility, reveal their own eras and resonate with historical information if we ask the right questions.

Although a painted or sculpted portrait often gives us a personal likeness, created through an intersection between artist and sitter, the poster portrait displays a public likeness. It is born of the interaction between the designer, the group or person commissioning the poster (such as a

Fig. 1. *La Bohème*. John Gilbert (1897–1936) by Batiste Madalena (1902–1989), tempera on board, 1926. National Portrait Gallery, Smithsonian Institution; gift of Judith and Steven Katten

federal agency, theatrical impresario, or film studio), and the celebrity image being exploited or promoted. Thus Batiste Madalena's posters of the silent-film stars Colleen Moore in *Lilac Time* (p. 65) or John Gilbert in *La Bohème* (fig. 1) are not the result of the artist's experiencing the personalities of the sitters through portrait sittings or performance. Rather, they were initiated by George Eastman's desire to elevate the status of moving pictures by using hand-painted posters in the ornate brass cases on the exterior of his Rochester, New York, movie palace. Madalena's image of Moore advertised the film by highlighting her bobbed-haired-look face, and enhanced the design with diving airplanes and the crisp, geometric style much favored in 1920s advertising art. It did not matter that she was cast as a curly-haired country girl in *Lilac Time;* her public knew her as a chic young urban flapper. The poster's suggestion of fast-paced contemporary fashion would sell Moore's new movie. Poster portraits, in other words, help us to understand the preconceived public image inherent in famous faces—how individuals were promoted and perceived.

Poster art is a form of communication that has roots in antiquity. Painted announcements and proclamations were found on the walls of Pompeii; the Romans used poster-like signs to advertise gladiator fights and chariot races. But it was the increasing urbanization of the Industrial Revolution that set the scene for the printed poster to flourish. By the early nineteenth century, broadsides, theater handbills and proliferating product advertisements joined the lettered and pictorial signage of shops and taverns to create an urban street literature of announcements and promotions. The *$100,000 Reward* broadside (p. 30) demonstrates the effectiveness of bold Victorian typefaces and such pictorial elements as the pointing finger in this type of advertising, while the photographs of Lincoln's assassins mounted at the top transform it into a prototype of the "wanted" poster. As technological improvements in presses, printing, and papermaking made possible large sizes, vibrant colors, and an array of pictorial effects, the modern poster began to evolve.

In America, well before the Civil War, wood-engraved advertisements for circuses, minstrel acts, acrobats, magicians, and various traveling shows—printed in large, multi-sheet sizes with solid blocks of color—dominated other types of posted advertising, signaling the direction of poster art. Alfred S. Seer's large wood engraving of Thomas Edison (p. 33) is part of this stock show-poster tradition. In 1878, five hundred examples of Edison's newly invented phonograph were manufactured for exhibition under the auspices of a lyceum bureau, an organization that produced uplifting or educational programs for touring around the country. The poster, featuring Edison and his talking machine, announces a demonstration of the invention, providing a blank space at the top for the specifics of time and place. The wording beneath the image—"It Talks! It Sings! It Laughs! It Plays Cornet Songs"—promotes the remarkable feats of the phonograph with circus-style rhetoric. While advertising the event and the invention (which was substantially redesigned before it became commercially viable), the poster also publicizes the man behind it. Edison did not accompany his machines on the lyceum tour. He hardly needed

to when such a large and colorful poster kept his image and his accomplishments in the public eye.

As poster printing evolved from wood engraving to brightly colored lithography after the Civil War, it was employed to advertise many different products. But the circus still dominated the industry. About two weeks before the show arrived in town, an advance team of bill-posters arrived with their "paper," using as many as 5,000 to 8,000 pieces to blanket the area with enticing pictures of wild animals and daring feats. The circus, usually in town for only one day, depended heavily on posters to draw an audience and spent a considerable portion of its budget on this form of advertising. A certain element of exaggeration was expected as part of the lure, but no matter how extraordinary the act—like "the Celebrated Comic Rajade Troupe in a Graduated Line" in a Strobridge Company poster (p. 34)—the faces of the famous circus proprietors were an equally important part of the promotion in such a competitive industry. The framed heads of P. T. Barnum and James Bailey, with their then-partner James Hutchinson, are as enticing a promise of the fun to come as the stilts-walking band.

Despite the beauty and drama of the charging buffalo in the poster *I Am Coming* (p. 46) it needed the head of Colonel William F. "Buffalo Bill" Cody to be effective advertising. The poster announced the imminent arrival of Cody's Wild West Show, a part circus, part rodeo extravaganza that grafted authentic western traditions onto preconceived myths and historical reenactments. By 1900, Cody's recognizable face, nickname, and reputation could sell the performance. So, in contrast to the busy circus posters, this image delivers its message with elegant simplicity. Each of the three main components— portrait, animal, and three-word title—enhances the others, and the viewer absorbs all three with immediate recognition.

As American circus and wild west shows traveled abroad, so did their poster art. The French artist Jules Chéret is said to have been influenced by American wood-engraved circus posters that he saw in England, where he was studying improvements in color printing. Returning to France in the late

1860s to start his own lithographic printing press, he began producing exuberant posters of Parisian nightlife, the success of which helped launch an international poster craze in the late nineteenth century. In 1893, he was one of many artists who attempted to capture the visual illusion that American dancer Loïe Fuller created (p. 37). Using rich, warm hues and printing separate versions of the poster in different shades, Chéret captured Fuller's dynamic performance and the brilliant effect of the changing multicolored electric lights on her costume.

The artists of this poster-mad era incorporated new decorative styles into their designs, including a fluid art nouveau aesthetic and the dark contour lines, flat areas of color, and angled viewpoints inspired by Japanese woodblock prints. These posters, proliferating on the streets of Paris, initiated a frenzy of interest that generated collectors, specialized dealers, exhibitions, and publications. The craze spread throughout Europe and England, resulting in a profusion of styles. The fad increased the emphasis on artistic design in all commercial art and advertising. The integration of fine and applied arts would have far-reaching implications for twentieth-century graphic design.

The vogue for artistic, or "picture," posters, as they were called, reached the United States in the 1890s, stimulated primarily by the publishing industry. When Edward Penfield, a young art editor at *Harper's* magazine, started designing posters to advertise each issue of the monthly periodical, he started a trend. Publishers began to hire leading artists and illustrators to produce poster advertising for magazines, books, and newspapers. William Sergeant Kendall's 1895 poster advertised an issue of *Scribner's* monthly magazine that included an article on the painter Robert Blum (p. 38). This simplified portrait image, with its stark composition and angled viewpoint, impressed one contemporary critic as resembling a "telegraph utterance, short, nervous, incisive." The work of Edward Penfield was in such great demand that he created a specialty item for collectors, his *Poster Calendar 1897,* with a self-portrait on the cover (p. 41). The opposing diagonals, flat areas of color, spattered background, and limited palette of orange, yellow, green, and black exemplified Penfield's approach, in which a quiet mood is invigorated by vivacious design.

The poster craze and the resulting collecting frenzy transformed a throwaway piece of commercial ephemera into a work of fine art with perceived artistic and monetary value. Posters have been blurring the boundaries between fine, popular, and commercial art with dizzying regularity ever since. The aestheticizing influence of the late nineteenth century, for example, crept into the designs of the large commercial lithography companies. The anonymous artists of the theatrical posters for Lillian Russell and Ada Rehan (pp. 42, 45) consciously incorporated decorative elements to heighten the appeal of their leading ladies. Advertising executives would later reject contemporary fine-art styles as ineffective for posters, arguing for a plain, unembellished approach. For this generation, however, a decorative style not only promoted the show or sold the magazine, it added an aura of contemporary fashion to the portrayed subject.

If the artistic posters of the 1890s show influence from abroad, much posted advertising also tells the story of the exportation of American culture. Jules Chéret was influenced by American circus advertisements and Loïe Fuller's theatrical lighting. The Buffalo Bill poster bears a French tax stamp and was apparently intended to promote one of Cody's enormously successful European tours (a French version of the image bears the translated caption "Je Viens"). A Belgian poster of renowned American cyclist Marshall ("Major") Taylor (p. 49) and a German image of the first black heavyweight champion, Jack Johnson (p. 50), suggest the international appeal of sporting events and the universal admiration for great athletes that would become such an important part of twentieth-century global culture. These posters tell us the story of international cultural exchange at the dawn of the century.

The decorative influence of the late nineteenth century poster artists has disappeared in the 1902 advertisement for cyclist Major Taylor. Nonetheless, the emphatic double portrait and rich, dark skin tones against the bright background present a commanding invitation to the event it advertised. The poster of heavyweight boxer Jack Johnson, from around 1910, an equally direct representation, does not announce a personal appearance but a film of the controversial fight between Johnson and the white pugilist Jim Jeffries. The bitter racial overtones of the match, which caused race riots in the United States when Jeffries was soundly defeated, have disappeared altogether in the German poster, which shows only admiration for a superb athlete. The absence of racial prejudice in these celebratory European pictures throws into stark relief the omnipresent implication of racial inferiority in America at the time.

Posters were playing an increasingly important role in the urban culture. The fledgling film industry, developing at about the same moment, saw their potential as a primary form of advertising. Mary Pickford's ringlets (fig. 2) and Charlie Chaplin's "little tramp" attire (p. 57), depicted in posters by Danish artist Sven Brasch, had universal recognition and helped to establish the movies' growing dominance worldwide. Since the industry produced a great quantity of short films in the early days, it came to rely on the stars' established characterizations to bring audiences back to the theater repeatedly.

The poster of Buster Keaton by French artist Jean-Albert Mercier (p. 66), which utilizes unusual colors and contemporary art deco geometric forms for effect, also features two well-known aspects of the comedian's performance: his mask-like, expressionless face and his portrayal of the individual's struggle against mechanical forces.

The United States government had made little use of motion pictures prior to World War I. But George Creel, who headed the Committee on Public Information (CPI), began producing such films as *Pershing's Crusaders* (p. 54), which he considered crucial for encouraging the war effort at home and building goodwill overseas. Enormous posters publicized the official screenings of *Pershing's Crusaders* in twenty-four American cities. European releases for popular American movies starring Charlie Chaplin or Mary Pickford were often paired with the showing of such CPI films. General Pershing's appeal could not match that of Chaplin or Pickford, but an inspirational poster casting him in the role of a crusader on a religious mission was effective government propaganda. In hindsight, it reveals an assumption of universal adherence to Christianity and an age-old reliance on religion to justify wartime actions.

Creel considered posters a critical medium for wartime

Fig. 2. *Stakkels Johanne (Johanna Enlists).* Mary Pickford (1893–1979) by Sven Brasch (1886–1970), linocut poster, 1921. National Portrait Gallery, Smithsonian Institution

communication. "I had the conviction," he wrote, "that the poster must play a great part in the fight for public opinion. The printed word might not be read, people might not choose to attend meetings or to watch motion pictures, but the billboard was something that caught even the most indifferent eye." Creel asked Charles Dana Gibson to recruit a volunteer committee of artists to help supply the government's poster needs. The Division of Pictorial Publicity, launched in April 1917, recruited painters, illustrators, and cartoonists and opened headquarters in Boston, Chicago, New York, and San Francisco. The division's mission, according to artist Cass Gilbert, was "to place upon every wall in America the call to patriotism and to service." Few of the artists were experienced poster designers, but such images as K. M. Bara's *You Are Wanted By U.S. Army* (p. 53), with its limited color scheme, dramatic equestrian portrait, and rather awkward integration of words, did their best to infuse higher forms of art into the patriotic message.

After the war, another rearing horse and a similarly simplified color palette promoted the great cowboy actor William S. Hart (p. 61). The poster was produced in Stockholm in 1922 for Hart's film *O'Malley of the Mounted,* which the Swedes re-titled *Brother of the Lightning.* One of the first film stars of the American western, Hart was so well known that the poster artist did not have to depict his face; the lean silhouette, tall cowboy hat, and gun were instantly familiar, even to a foreign audience. American films were typically advertised by poster art made in the country that imported them. The stylized face of Fredric March, for example, morphs into his evil doppelganger in the Swedish poster for *Dr. Jekyll and Mr. Hyde* (p. 70). Like magazine advertising of the 1920s, many posters of this period reflected a simplified, sharp-lined "modern" style, whose geometry, asymmetry, and fashionable distortion seemed to imply a sophisticated urban tempo. The foreign posters generally conform to the celebrity images so carefully honed by the American actors and their studios, helping us chart the reputations of these individuals as they spread internationally. The iconic faces of Greta Garbo (p. 73) and Marlene Dietrich (fig. 3), for example,

Fig. 3. *Den Røde Kejserinde (The Scarlet Empress)*. Marlene Dietrich (1901–1992) by W. Palle (active c. 1930–1945), color lithographic poster, 1934. National Portrait Gallery, Smithsonian Institution

dominate the advertising for the German release of *Queen Christina* and the Danish release of *The Scarlet Empress*.

Design trends gradually began to move away from modernist art and toward straight photography for advertising and magazine illustration of the 1930s. Photographic faces add immediacy and impact to a 1932 Shell Oil poster (p. 69), which inserts images of popular aviators Jimmy Doolittle and Jimmy Haizlip into a newspaper "extra." This clever conceit promoted the Shell name with the urgency of late-breaking news. According to the poster, the two renowned stunt fliers were actually "flying for Shell" in various competitions at the time. Their ability to "smash all records" was, by extension, attributable to the superiority of the company and its products.

Since the nineteenth century, famous figures had been used for product advertising, and such testimonials increased dramatically in the 1920s, in both magazines and on the radio. As the president of the J. Walter Thompson advertising firm pointed out, there was ample evidence that people wanted their "news, education, and entertainment conveyed . . . through the medium of personalities." When celebrity endorsement was enlarged from page to poster size, the effect could be dramatic. Billie Burke, along with other stage and screen beauties, was recruited to advertise Lux soap (fig. 4). The drama of this large-scale image was the pairing of her glowing face with her signed quote, "I'm 39." Her true age—forty-six at the time the poster campaign was probably launched—might have been even more effective. In the 1940s, two different soap companies, Lux and Wood-bury, chose Paramount film star Veronica Lake to advertise their facial products. The stand-up poster for "Woodbury Matched Make-up" (p. 86) downplays Lake's signature "peekaboo" hair style as well as the the-atrical lighting of much film promotion to render a full view of her oval face and perfect complexion. The poster mar-kets the products and extends her reputation as a Hollywood leading lady. But the image also reminds us of the power of the film industry to influence and update female standards of beauty, which at that moment emphasized plucked, penciled brows and bright red lips.

During World War II, film clips, leaflets, and radio broad-casting were all employed to communicate with the Ameri-can public. Nonetheless, all the military branches, along with such agencies as the FBI, the Treasury, and the Office of Defense Transportation, still found posters to be effective propaganda tools. The Office of War Information, which attempted to coordinate all poster production, emphasized the unembellished photograph-ic imagery, uncomplicated messages, and short, simple texts favored by commercial advertisers at the time. Al-though most posters featured generic figures, Treasury bond and industrial incentive cam-paigns often used such re-nowned personalities as Admiral William F. Halsey (p. 74) or Admiral Chester Nimitz to inspire the home front (fig. 5). Eschewing mod-ern art, sophisticated design, stylish lettering, or symbolic subtlety, these posters substi-tuted manly images of a gen-eral or admiral, cloaking their propaganda with patriotism. The public's eternal "search for authority," cited by one adver-tising executive, seemed to have even more resonance during wartime. Although many poster designers exploited sentimental themes related to

Fig. 4. *"I'm 39. . . . "* Billie Burke (1884–1970) by an unidentified artist, color photolithographic poster, c. 1930–32. National Portrait Gallery, Smithsonian Institution

Laugh at Birthdays as 9 out of 10 Screen Stars do ..use

Lux Toilet Soap

"I'm 39.."

Billie Burke

the family and American values, these pieces delivered the authoritative voices of military leaders uniting the home front and the battle front under a single command.

A different tone—once again religious and inspirational—is evident in the World War II poster that features boxer Joe Louis with the quoted caption, "We're going to do our part . . . and we will win because we're on God's side" (p. 78). Portraits of the popular heavyweight champion, a hero for many in the black community, were frequently on display in the 1930s. This simply designed but effective image, like the poster of Navy messman Dorie Miller (p. 81), was issued for general morale-building purposes. The "Negro Desk" at the Office of War Information, keenly aware of the need to provide the heroes and role models that black Americans were not finding in the general press, lobbied tirelessly on behalf of more recognition for black achievements. Much World War II poster art implies a unified national cause. The Louis and Miller posters remind us of those excluded from that norm, who required their own campaign just to encourage morale.

Fig. 5. *Give Us The Stuff And We'll Hit It!* Chester Nimitz (1885–1966) by John Philip Falter (1910–1982), color photolithographic poster with halftone, 1944. National Portrait Gallery, Smithsonian Institution; gift of Leslie, Judith, and Gabri Schreyer and Alice Schreyer Batko

The photographic realism of wartime advertising spilled over into 1950s film promotion. American posters of the time were often a montage of film stills, with little aesthetic ambition. Some posters, however, infused this usually unimaginative genre with a playful touch. The poster for the 20th Century-Fox film *Niagara* (p. 98), for instance, places star Marilyn Monroe reclining sexily on top of the falls. The reference to mythic traditions relating water and female sexuality to regeneration and rebirth was clearly unintentional; the humor of the overblown rhetoric—"Marilyn Monroe and *Niagara* / a raging torrent of emotion that even nature can't control!"—undoubtedly was. *Niagara,* like the circus posters of the nineteenth century, used rhetoric and visual exaggeration to entice its audience. The same studio's poster of a dazzling Dorothy Dandridge for the film adaptation of the opera *Carmen* (p. 101) provided one of the most compelling American film advertisements of the era. The nearly life-size figure, radiating vitality, beauty, and defiance, combined with the music-sheet background and primary colors to give the poster a vivacity others could not match. These posters promoted neither the woman nor the character she played but the constructed image the movie producers wanted to market.

The film-still montage of most American posters was transformed in post–World War II Italy, where the poster industry enjoyed a revival in the 1950s. The enormous posters, based on painted renditions of the stars' photographic images, are visually arresting. Such artists as Anselmo Ballester or Ercole Brini revitalized their mundane sources with large scale and dramatic hues. Brini's painterly portrait of Cary Grant and Grace Kelly on the poster for *To Catch a Thief* (fig. 6) was based on a movie still from a particularly dramatic, sexually charged scene in the film. The artist added a green glove and a black cat, a reference to Grant's "cat burglar" character, and surrounded the image with an unexpected turquoise border and bold yellow lettering. Ballester's poster for *Affair in Trinidad* (p. 94) combines a vivacious portrait of Rita Hayworth in color with a menacing image of Glenn Ford in black and white, attracting attention through the startling disjunction of mood between the two. The flame-haired goddess of the poster also reinforces Hayworth's studio-enforced transformation from a dark-haired Spanish beauty into a pale-skinned

CARY GRANT

GRACE KELLY

un film di ALFRED HITCHCOCK

È un film Paramount

CACCIA AL LADRO

(TO CATCH A THIEF)

CON JESSIE ROYCE LANDIS · JOHN WILLIAMS
REGIA DI
ALFRED HITCHCOCK · JOHN MICHAEL HAYES
SCENEGGIATURA DI

UNA PRODUZIONE IN

VISTAVISION

COLORE DELLA
TECHNICOLOR

TRATTO DALL'OMONIMO ROMANZO DI D. DODGE PUBBLICATO IN ITALIA DA CINO DEL DUCA EDITORE

Hollywood idol, reflecting the era's prejudice toward northern European ancestry.

No posters are more concerned with building upon or establishing public images than political campaign advertising. James Montgomery Flagg's poster for Franklin Delano Roosevelt's 1944 presidential campaign (p. 85) marries two iconic images: the artist's famous "I Want You" drawing of Uncle Sam from World War I and the president's well-recognized face. Few American poster designs were as renowned as Flagg's early recruiting placard, which was based on a self-portrait. His appropriation, years later, of the much-imitated, finger-pointing Uncle Sam no doubt intrigued viewers while suggesting that their support for FDR was nothing less than a patriotic gesture. While a recognizable face might seem a necessary component for political imagery, Ben Shahn's poster for the 1948 election (p. 89) avoids both the face and the name of

Henry A. Wallace, the Progressive Party's candidate, choosing instead to satirize Democrat Harry Truman and Republican Thomas Dewey. Campaign managers, however, generally preferred simple, unimaginative poster imagery to promote their candidates. Barry Goldwater's 1964 campaign stuck with photographic faces of the candidate and his running mate, depending only on large scale and a bold golden-colored background to secure attention (p. 102).

The 1960s revolutionized the design, purpose, and collecting of posters, turning low-cost advertising products into decorative statements of one's personal affiliations and launching a second poster craze. As images of film celebrities, rock bands, and political activism wallpapered dorm rooms within the rapidly expanding collegiate demographic, poster vendors flourished, and the press took notice. *Life* magazine called the phenomenon "The Big Poster Hang-Up" in 1967; Hilton Kramer called it "Postermania" in a 1968 commentary in the *New York Times;* and "Pop Goes the Poster" was the title of Herbert Gold's 1968

Fig. 6. *Caccia al Ladro (To Catch a Thief).* Cary Grant (1904–1986) and Grace Kelly (1929–1982) by Ercole Brini (1913–1989), color halftone and lithographic poster, c. 1955. National Portrait Gallery, Smithsonian Institution

article for the *Saturday Evening Post.* The lowly poster, Gold noted, became the "son of button, big brother of the bumper sticker, weird indoor stepcousin of the billboard, teeny-bopper daughter of the painting, city-slicker cousin of the print." More than a million posters a week, *Life* reported, are "gobbled up by avid visual maniacs." Personality and protest posters were often dramatic photographic images. "Wellesley girls prefer Paul Newmans over their beds," *Newsweek* reported in the March 6, 1967, issue. The photographic poster of Huey Newton, the "Minister of Defence" for the Black Panthers (p. 125), posed with a gun, a spear, and African shields, quickly became an iconic protest image.

While celebrity and activist images could be photographic, much of the poster art of the 1960s sported a radical new look. On the East Coast, the disparate artists of New York's Push Pin Studios promoted innovation, ignoring Bauhaus-inspired spareness and turning toward such aesthetic precursors as Victorian, art nouveau, and American primitive styles. "Stylistic complacency and platitudinous thinking" were the common enemies, accord-

ing to one commentator, for such innovative Push Pin artists as Milton Glaser, Seymour Chwast, Ed Sorel, and Paul Davis. "All the things that the doctrine of orthodox modernism seemed to have contempt for—ornamentation, narrative illustration, visual ambiguity—attracted us," Milton Glaser claimed. His *Dylan* (p. 106), a giveaway insert for the 1967 album *Bob Dylan's Greatest Hits,* quickly became another icon of the era. Glaser claimed to be influenced by a famous silhouette profile by Marcel Duchamp and the jewel-like colors of Islamic art.

Young Americans particularly liked the images that "jolt the eye, or make the mind go topsy-turvy," according to *Life.* The magazine's description of the "psychedelicacies of almost fluorescent oranges and lavender" referred to the intensely colored, mid-1960s West Coast rock posters designed by Wes Wilson, Victor Moscoso, and others advertising Bill Graham's programs for San Francisco's Fillmore Auditorium (pp. 109, 110, 113). Wes Wilson recalled selecting his colors from his hallucinatory experiences with LSD. The illegibility of Wilson's odd lettering, quickly imitated by other designers, frustrated Graham. But this innovative style successfully evoked the burgeoning counterculture and spawned avid poster collecting throughout the Bay Area, across the nation, and overseas.

The collectible poster trend launched in the 1960s continued strongly into the next two decades. Darien House, one company that capitalized on the student fad for displaying inexpensive posters with a contemporary look, commissioned advertising but also distributed to poster vendors the overruns of their own—and others'—poster art. Such Darien images as Richard Amsel's 1973 *Bette Midler* (p. 130), Paul Davis's 1977 *We Are Still Here* (p. 133), featuring Native American activist Leonard Crow Dog, and Avi Farin's 1979 *Dizzy Gillespie Quintet* (fig. 7) offered collectors a jazzy, contemporary look.

Photographic celebrity portraits were the key component for an enormously successful advertising campaign for Blackglama mink coats. Concerned about a decline in the popularity of fur garments in the 1960s, an association of mink producers turned to a New York advertiser to create an attention-getting new approach. Launched in 1968, the stark black–and–white posters featured Richard Avedon's photographs of such recognizable personalities as Bette Davis and Judy Garland (pp. 114, 117), each garbed in her own choice of coat. Combined with the caption "What becomes a Legend most?" the campaign was wildly successful. Not only did the intersection of photography, celebrity, luxury, and glamour serve the purpose of commerce, it also produced collectible art: a high-style version of the personality poster. The campaign continued with such pictures as a high-kicking Shirley MacLaine with photographs by Bill King (p. 118).

The younger generation saw musicians as lifestyle and fashion role models. Their avid interest in the recording industry helped spur the fad for collecting and displaying innovative poster art. The 1970 capsule-shaped *Winner?* poster depicting Janis Joplin and Jimi Hendrix (p. 126), produced shortly after their tragic deaths, pushed against the youthful trend for modeling behavior on the drug-infused world of contemporary rock music. With equal graphic power, the photographic poster of Grace Jones, advertising her 1981 *Grace Jones/ Nightclubbing* album (p. 142), confirmed her defining look. The defiant, androgynous figure suggests not only new trends in fashion but a chic conflation of gender stereotypes and more liberal attitudes toward sexual difference.

From the 1960s on, the poster seesawed from powerful photographic imagery to sleek, strong graphic design. In the latter category, Niklaus Troxler's large advertisement for a Thelonious Monk tribute concert ingeniously outlines the jazz icon's recognizable profile with bright, primary-colored words (p. 145). Although quite different in scale and design, Michael Schwab's poster of renowned Tour de France cyclist Lance Armstrong (p. 149), commissioned by helmetmaker Giro Sport Design, also employs the drama of a simple profile and the appeal of primary colors. Here used symbolically, the colors are not only patriotic but suggestive of the tour leader's jersey and the yellow "livestrong" wristbands of Armstrong's cancer-fighting foundation. As in Milton Glaser's *Dylan* poster, the five-letter name is integrated seamlessly into the design.

The accessibility and popularity of the poster also intrigued such artists from the fine-art world as Larry Rivers, who produced an advertisement for presidential hopeful George McGovern (p. 129), and Robert Rauschenberg, who designed a celebratory placard for the AFL/CIO labor organization (p. 141). Should posters produced with commercial printing techniques sell at the same prices that work by those artists typically commands? The question, and the confusion it suggests, only underscores the poster's ongoing ability to blur or transcend boundaries of high and low culture.

Advertising turned to other formats at the end of the twentieth century, and the impact of the poster lost its primacy as a ubiquitous urban presence and a statement of one's personal affiliations. But television and the Internet fueled the national obsession with the famous in the 1990s. Increased exposure subtly shifted the parameters of celebrity, creating a faux intimacy and familiarity that gave new commercial potential to

Fig. 7. *Dizzy Gillespie Quintet*. Dizzy Gillespie (1917–1993) by Avi Farin (born 1943), color photolithographic halftone poster, 1979. National Portrait Gallery, Smithsonian Institution; gift of Jack Rennert

DIZZY GILLESPIE QUINTET

art blakey & the jazz messengers · aug 28–sep 91

Varin 79

At Art D'Lugoff's

VILLAGE GATE

the face of an athlete or film star. The bizarre, humorous, and very successful milk-mustache advertising posters reflect this marketing power. Launched in the mid-1990s by milk processors who hoped to reverse declining sales by targeting adults, the "Got Milk?" campaign (as it later became known) is undeniably playful. Annie Leibovitz's clever photographs made every famous face and beautiful body ridiculous. The advertising agency's creative director initially thought that famous subjects in advertising had been "overused" in the previous two decades. But the humor of the campaign gave celebrity endorsement a fresh, anti-glamour informality that implied an intimate connection with those depicted. Tennis champion Pete Sampras was one of many who wanted to be subjects and even sent the advertising agency a milk mustache image of himself. In the poster, Sampras is bare-torsoed, with a towel tossed over his head as if he were headed to the showers (p. 146). But he reveals nothing of his tennis skills. He seems instead an example of the achievement-free celebrity of the 1990s, a commercially viable commodity more for his

recognizable name and toned physique than his athletic ranking. These images update the distanced, glamorized celebrity of the Blackglama ads.

Dramatic, and often enormous, likenesses on posters hardly seem subtle, but in fact, what a poster communicates about an individual is usually secondary to its principal message: selling war bonds, announcing the coming of a circus, advertising a product, or publicizing a film. Thus the portrait image can be a subliminal visual statement for the viewer, not focused upon but absorbed. Some advertising we invite, in a sense, by picking up a magazine or turning on a television. Posters are insistent, unsolicited visual messages that are familiar aspects of our environment. When they depict public figures, we record the images they present subconsciously, with little awareness of how they operate in establishing or solidifying fame.

How does the audience for poster advertising receive these dramatic visual messages? That is the wrong question to ponder, for we rarely find an answer. Instead we can ask how posters reflect cultural norms at any given moment. Their designers intend to manipulate and persuade. But if we are sensitive to the makers' obvious intentions, posters can open a window through which we can see the attitudes of their era. Like other forms of advertising and popular art, posters draw upon prevailing ideals, presumptions, and prejudices. Even the most innovative of their designers must provide accessible imagery and a clear message; they inevitably borrow from shared generational perceptions that we can identify in hindsight. Thus we can probe these poster portraits for attitudes about gender roles, racial complexities, idealized forms of femininity and masculinity, sexual boundaries, feelings about our celebrity idols, wartime emotions of patriotism and complicity, or passionate rebellion.

Throughout its history, the poster has proven to be remarkably flexible as an art form, adapting in each generation to emerging graphic styles, different industries, fresh marketing strategies, and new passions. A life-size stand-up poster of Johnny Depp as Captain Jack Sparrow from *Pirates of the Caribbean* (p. 150), or the same image in a banner two stories tall, still captures our attention, underscoring how completely Depp's antic performance defined the film trilogy while adding an entertaining note to our visual surroundings. Is it art, or popular culture, or mere commerce? The poster's uncategorizable status adds to its roguish appeal but should not prevent us from reading its varied messages intelligently. Portraiture has never been restricted to the fine-art world. Widely disseminated popular forms of portraiture like the poster remain a profound influence. As the urban/suburban divide transforms itself into a widespread metropolitan culture, we must learn to read the visual cues that surround us.

The Posters

SURRAT.   BOOTH.   HAROLD.

War Department, Washington, April 20, 1865,

 # $100,000 REWARD!

THE MURDERER

Of our late beloved President, Abraham Lincoln,

IS STILL AT LARGE.

$50,000 REWARD

Will be paid by this Department for his apprehension, in addition to any reward offered by Municipal Authorities or State Executives.

$25,000 REWARD

Will be paid for the apprehension of JOHN H. SURRATT, one of Booth's Accomplices.

$25,000 REWARD

Will be paid for the apprehension of David C. Harold, another of Booth's accomplices.

LIBERAL REWARDS will be paid for any information that shall conduce to the arrest of either of the above-named criminals, or their accomplices.

All persons harboring or secreting the said persons, or either of them, or aiding or assisting their concealment or escape, will be treated as accomplices in the murder of the President and the attempted assassination of the Secretary of State, and shall be subject to trial before a Military Commission and the punishment of DEATH.

Let the stain of innocent blood be removed from the land by the arrest and punishment of the murderers.

All good citizens are exhorted to aid public justice on this occasion. Every man should consider his own conscience charged with this solemn duty, and rest neither night nor day until it be accomplished.

EDWIN M. STANTON, Secretary of War.

DESCRIPTIONS.—BOOTH is Five Feet 7 or 8 inches high, slender build, high forehead, black hair, black eyes, and wears a heavy black moustache.

JOHN H. SURRAT is about 5 feet, 9 inches. Hair rather thin and dark; eyes rather light; no beard. Would weigh 145 or 150 pounds. Complexion rather pale and clear, with color in his cheeks. Wore light clothes of fine quality. Shoulders square; cheek bones rather prominent; chin narrow; ears projecting at the top; forehead rather low and square, but broad. Parts his hair on the right side; neck rather long. His lips are firmly set. A slim man.

DAVID C. HAROLD is five feet six inches high, hair dark, eyes dark, eyebrows rather heavy, full face, nose short, hand short and fleshy, feet small, instep high, round bodied, naturally quick and active, slightly closes his eyes when looking at a person.

NOTICE.—In addition to the above, State and other authorities have offered rewards amounting to almost one hundred thousand dollars, making an aggregate of about TWO HUNDRED THOUSAND DOLLARS.

$100,000 Reward

John H. Surratt | 1844–1916
John Wilkes Booth | 1838–1865
David E. Herold | c. 1842–1865

Unidentified artist
Printed broadside with albumen silver prints, 1865
61.4 x 31.9 cm (24 3/16 x 12 9/16 in.)
National Portrait Gallery, Smithsonian Institution

The modern poster evolved from printed broadsides like this dramatic announcement of a "$100,000 Reward." Issued five days after President Abraham Lincoln's assassination at Ford's Theatre on April 14, 1865, this early form of the "wanted" poster promised money for the capture of John Wilkes Booth and two accomplices. After federal soldiers mortally wounded Booth in Caroline County, Virginia, and captured Herold, there was a clamor for the reward money, a portion of which was divided among the officers and twenty-six soldiers.

Posted broadsides, a common form of street literature in the nineteenth century, often featured modest wood engravings like the small pointing finger seen here. This image, however, attracts attention not only with bold, dark typefaces and actual photographs of the murderous gang but also with the combined psychological thrills of sensational criminality and a large monetary reward.

Edison's Phonograph

Thomas Edison | 1847–1931

Alfred S. Seer (active 1859–1900), after Mathew Brady
Color woodcut poster, c. 1878
209.2 x 105.3 cm (82 3/8 x 41 7/16 in.)
National Portrait Gallery, Smithsonian Institution

"It Talks! It Sings! It Laughs!" The startling assertions of this poster undoubtedly attracted the curious to demonstrations of Thomas Edison's newly invented phonograph. In 1878, after filing his patent, Edison went to Washington, where he had his portrait made at Mathew Brady's photography studio and showed off his "talking machine" at the Capitol, the White House, and the American Academy of Sciences. The same year, five hundred demonstration models of his phonograph toured around the country on the lyceum circuit.

This large wood-engraved poster, with a blank space over the Brady image for inserting the specific time and place for the demonstrations, is similar to the color posters that promoted circuses. It tells us more about the man than the machine, which was eventually redesigned. Far from being a lone genius, Edison was a famous personality, and his ability to stay in the public eye was an important factor in his career.

EDISON'S

A.S.SEER·ENG·PRINTING

PHONOGRAPH

OR TALKING MACHINE
IT TALKS! IT SINGS! IT LAUGHS!
IT PLAYS CORNET SONGS

P. T. Barnum's Greatest Show on Earth

P. T. Barnum | 1810–1891

James Bailey | 1847–1906

James L. Hutchinson | 1846–1910

Strobridge Lithography Company (active c. 1867–1961)
Chromolithographic poster, c. 1881–85
76.1 x 101.3 cm (29 15/16 x 39 7/8 in.)
National Portrait Gallery, Smithsonian Institution

No other industry in America was as dependent on poster advertising as the circus. The thousands of sheets of paper that appeared on every barn and fence in town shortly before the circus arrived were as much a part of the show as the parade and the performance. In bright colors and large sizes, circus posters easily dominated other forms of commercial advertising. This crowded poster by the Strobridge Lithography Company, renowned for its theater, show, and circus advertising, enticed the reader with multiple offerings. In addition to the delightful center illustration and promises of three circuses in rings, two menageries in tents, and seven monster shows, the poster lured viewers with portraits, printed in contrasting black and white, of the legendary proprietors, Phineas T. Barnum and James Bailey, and their partner at the time, James Hutchinson.

Folies-Bergère La Loïe Fuller

Loïe Fuller | 1862–1928

Jules Chéret (1836–1932)
Color lithographic poster, 1893
130.2 x 91.9 cm (51 1/4 x 36 3/16 in.)
National Portrait Gallery, Smithsonian Institution

The exuberant posters of Parisian nightlife that French artist Jules Chéret began producing in the 1860s helped launch an international poster craze in the late nineteenth century. Chéret was known for his brilliant colors—described by one critic as "a hooray of reds, a hallelujah of yellows and a primal scream of blues"—but the effects of his 1893 poster of American dancer Loïe Fuller were actually inspired by her own performance. The former Mary Louise Fuller of Fullersburg, Illinois, was the sensation of Paris at the time. Against a black velvet background, she focused changing colored lights on her voluminous costumes of iridescent silk, creating a magical effect of swirling color and light. In this poster, the fiery colors, spiraled pose, and jagged contours enhance the sense of movement, and the laughing, turning figure seems momentarily suspended in time and space.

ROBERT BLUM'S
GREAT DECORATIVE
PAINTING
IN
JANUARY
SCRIBNER'S

J. E. RHODES, NEW YORK.

Robert Blum's Great Decorative Painting in January Scribner's

Robert F. Blum | 1857–1903

William Sergeant Kendall (1869–1938)
Color relief poster with halftone, 1895
43.9 x 31.9 cm (17 5/16 x 12 9/16 in.)
National Portrait Gallery, Smithsonian Institution;
gift of Leslie, Judith, and Gabri Schreyer
and Alice Schreyer Batko

In 1893, when a young art editor at *Harper's* designed a poster in the decorative style of the European poster craze to announce an upcoming issue, the results launched a competition for stylish magazine advertising in America. William Sergeant Kendall made three monthly placards for *Scribner's,* including this January 1895 image of the painter Robert Blum. Kendall's use of an angled viewpoint and heavy, dark contours suggests the influence of Japanese prints. The effect was noted by a contemporary critic, who wrote in 1895 that Kendall's portraits were "a telegraph utterance, short, nervous, incisive, spoken with a dash and go which seem to imply 'I have not time to linger on the curves of those lips, on the turn of that eyebrow, and neither do you. . . . I have uttered the essential thought; you may fill in the rest.'" Instead of using the magazine's masthead, Kendall hand-lettered the text himself, balancing the off-center composition.

Poster Calendar 1897

Edward Penfield | 1866–1925

Self-portrait
Color lithograph, 1896
35.6 x 25.7 cm (14 x 10 1/8 in.)
National Portrait Gallery, Smithsonian Institution

In the mid-1890s, when publishers started commissioning posters from leading illustrators and artists instead of large lithographic printing firms, the artistic poster craze that had started in Paris was launched in America. Numerous commissions and exhibitions followed, enticing enthusiastic collectors and encouraging specialized dealers. So keen was the interest that there was even a demand for poster books, magazines, and calendars, such as this one by Edward Penfield. A deluxe edition for collectors, it includes four black-and-white lithographic proofs along with four color calendar pages. The cover, depicting the artist at work, uses the opposing diagonals of the figure and the cat to suggest the depth of his work space, while the areas of flat color add to the boldness of the design. Penfield's subtle humor is also evident: the cat, seemingly painted with those very inks it is eyeing so intently, appears ready to pounce on the uncorked bottles.

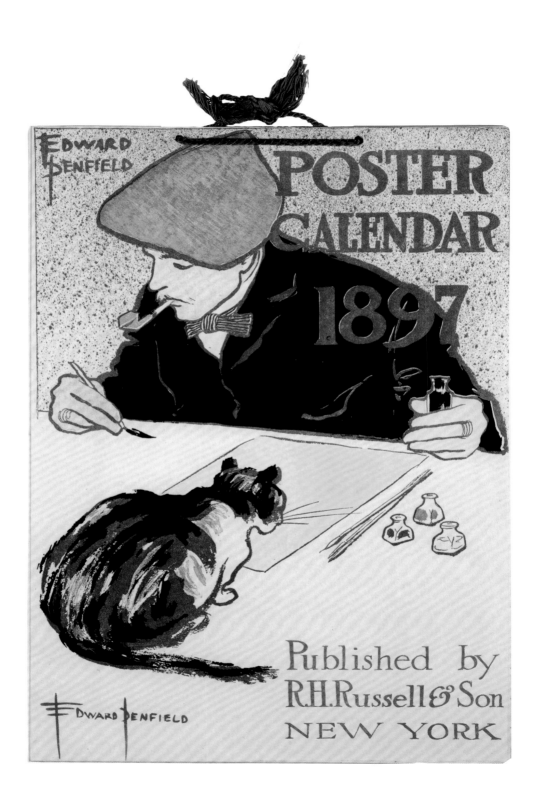

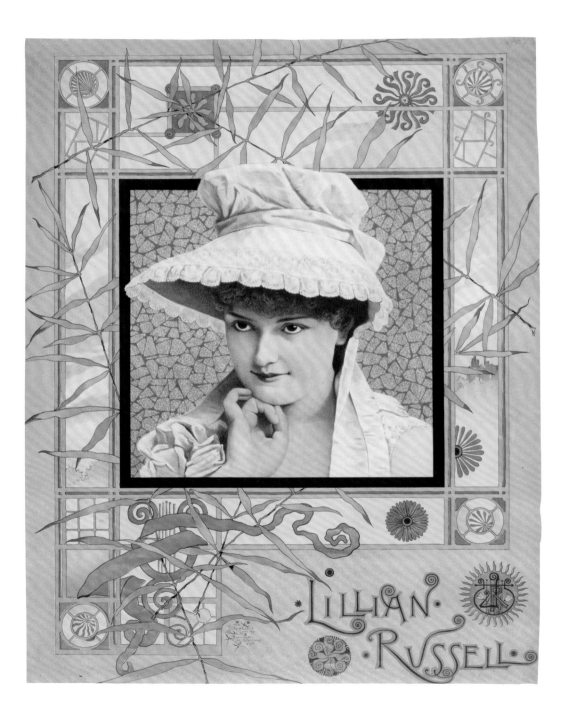

LILLIAN RUSSELL

Lillian Russell

Lillian Russell | 1861–1922

Strobridge Lithography Company (active c. 1867–1961)
Chromolithographic poster, c. 1890–95
79.7 x 60.6 cm (31 3/8 x 23 7/8 in.)
National Portrait Gallery, Smithsonian Institution

The enduring popularity of Lillian Russell as the prima donna of the American light opera stage had as much to do with her renowned beauty and flair for publicity as her voice and stage presence. The photographic face in this poster, suggesting the sweet and youthful heroines of Russell's many comic operas, is typical of late nineteenth-century commercial advertising. The elaborate ornamentation of the frame, however, and the subtle color stippling of the background show the influence of the French-inspired artistic poster movement on commercial printing firms in America. The unidentified artist from the Strobridge Lithography Company posed Russell's face against a marbleized wallpaper design within an elaborate frame inspired by contemporary stained glass and ornamented with bamboo fronds. The image is further embellished with an elegant monogram of initials, lilies, and a lyre, whose spiraling curls are echoed in the lettering of the name.

Miss Ada Rehan

Ada Rehan | 1857–1916

David Allen and Sons Ltd. Lithography Company
(active c. 1890s–1920s)
Chromolithographic poster, 1898
76.7 x 51.4 cm (30 3/16 x 20 1/4 in.)
National Portrait Gallery, Smithsonian Institution;
gift of Mr. and Mrs. Leslie J. Schreyer

The elegant decorative features of this commercially produced stock poster are reminiscent of 1890s wallpaper designs of stylized floral motifs and geometric patterns. With ornamental lettering to add to the effect, the poster is designed to promote the elegance and stature of Ada Rehan, a leading lady of the American stage, in any of her acclaimed roles. Here, the specifics of the performance are crudely stamped at the top of the poster, referring to her appearance at the Harlem Opera House on April 18, 1898, in *The Country Girl.* By that time, Rehan, a principal with Augustin Daly's famous company for nearly twenty years, had a loyal following. Actor Otis Skinner had once described her performance as "buoyant, scintillant, with a manner unlike other women, a voice that melted and caressed as it drawled, an awkward grace, an arch expression, a look of mischief in her gray Irish eyes."

I Am Coming
William F. "Buffalo Bill" Cody | 1846–1917

Courier Lithography Company (active c. 1882–1905)
Chromolithographic poster, 1900
76.2 x 110.8 cm (30 x 43 5/8 in.)
National Portrait Gallery, Smithsonian Institution

To a great promoter like Colonel William F. Cody, the semireligious phrase "I Am Coming" required larger letters on this poster than the identification of the face that everyone would already recognize. Cody, originally a frontier scout, Indian fighter, and buffalo hunter, had become famous as the hero of "Buffalo Bill" dime novels and magazine stories. In 1882, he created his popular wild west show and toured as its star for thirty years, arguably doing more than any single American to popularize the myth of the West. Combining sharpshooting, riding, and roping with historical reenactments of war dances, buffalo hunts, stagecoach attacks, and "Custer's Last Fight," Buffalo Bill's Wild West Show had enormous international appeal. In fact, this copy of the poster, bearing a French tax stamp (top right), is a testament to his extremely successful tours in France.

Major Taylor

Marshall W. "Major" Taylor | 1878–1932

Louis Galice (active c. 1887–1912)
Color lithographic poster with relief printing, 1902
130 x 93.5 cm (51 3/16 x 36 13/16 in.)
National Portrait Gallery, Smithsonian Institution

Marshall W. "Major" Taylor, the son of a coachman from Indianapolis, was the "fastest bicycle rider the world had ever known" when this poster was published in 1902. In the course of his sixteen-year career, Taylor competed in races throughout the United States, Canada, Europe, Australia, and New Zealand; won numerous championships; set several world records; and became one of the most glorified cyclists of the era when bicycling was an international craze. This Belgian poster, which advertises Taylor's appearance at a small fair at the Velodrome Zurenborg in Antwerp, avoids the decorative conceits of the renowned poster artists. Nonetheless, with its emphatic double image, brilliant yellow background, and red, white, and blue accents, it is a visually compelling announcement of the appearance of an athlete who, despite overt discrimination, "gained all the triumphs, gold, and glory possible to obtain" in his sport.

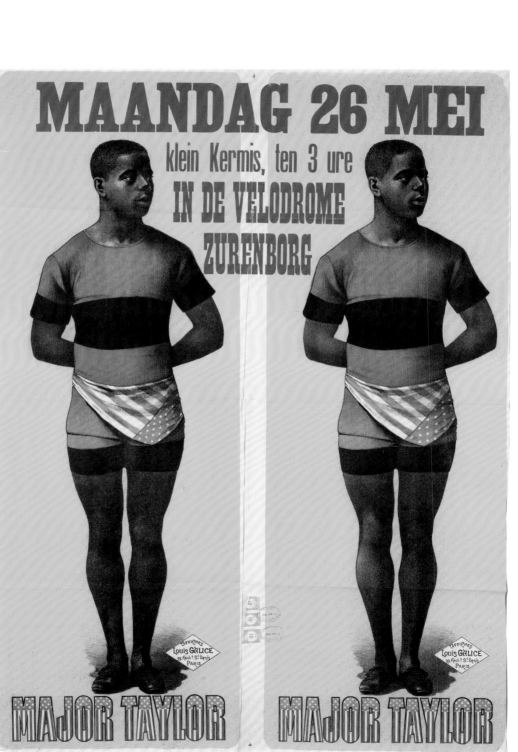

Champion-Match Johnson–Jeffries
Jack Johnson | 1878–1946

Adolph Friedländer Lithography Company (active 1872–1938)
Color lithographic poster, c. 1910
99.7 x 71.3 cm (39 1/4 x 28 1/16 in.)
National Portrait Gallery, Smithsonian Institution

This German poster portrays Jack Johnson, the first black world heavyweight boxing champion, as a dignified athlete of magnificent physique. Advertising a film of his 1910 fight with Jim Jeffries, the image avoids the controversies the bout caused in the United States. Social reformers, who viewed the sport as barbaric, were successful in moving the event from San Francisco to Reno. The match, pitting "the Negroes' Deliverer" against the "Hope of the White Race," engendered bitter racial overtones. Upsetting notions of white racial superiority, Johnson's decisive victory caused race riots around the country, and the film was banned in many American cities. Without reference to such tensions, this poster, produced by a Hamburg company known for its circus advertising, heralds the emergence of sporting events as a major entertainment industry in twentieth-century global culture.

You Are Wanted by U.S. Army

John J. Pershing | 1860–1948

K. M. Bara (active 1910s)
Color lithographic poster, c. 1917
106.7 x 72.5 cm (42 x 28 9/16 in.)
National Portrait Gallery, Smithsonian Institution

During World War I, posters seemed to promise a fast, efficient medium for communicating with the home front, and painters, cartoonists, and illustrators volunteered their artistic talents as a patriotic gesture. California artist K. M. Bara's *You Are Wanted by U.S. Army* recruiting poster depicted General John Joseph Pershing, the renowned commander of the American Expeditionary Force. Because of two famous advertising campaigns—Uncle Sam's "I Want You for the U.S. Army" and Lord Kitchener's "Your Country Needs You" in England—the pointing or outstretched hand became a frequent motif for poster propaganda during the war. In addition to that exhorting gesture, Bara used bold coloring and a lively composition of crossing diagonals with the upward-charging horse and the twisting figure. For those who missed the reference to a famous equestrian portrait—*Napoleon Crossing the Alps* by Jacques-Louis David—Pershing's recognizable figure was authoritative all on its own.

OFFICIAL U.S. WAR FILM
RELEASED BY
COMMITTEE ON PUBLIC
INFORMATION
GEORGE CREEL, CHAIRMAN

PERSHING'S CRUSADERS

AUSPICES OF THE

UNITED STATES GOVERNMENT

THE FIRST OFFICIAL AMERICAN WAR PICTURE

TAKEN BY
U.S. SIGNAL CORPS AND NAVY
PHOTOGRAPHERS

▼

Pershing's Crusaders
John J. Pershing | 1860–1948

H. C. Miner Lithography Company (active 1896–1935)
Color lithographic poster, 1918
200 x 104 cm (78 3/4 x 40 15/16 in.)
National Portrait Gallery, Smithsonian Institution

Up until World War I, the United States government had made little use of moving pictures, but by war's end the Committee on Public Information (CPI), headed by George Creel, considered its Division of Films crucial for wartime propaganda. This 1918 poster advertises the division's first feature-length film based on military footage, *Pershing's Crusaders,* which was screened in twenty-four cities in theaters decorated with flags and bunting. Inspirational posters like this one, equating General John J. Pershing and his troops with crusaders on a religious mission, helped to publicize the screenings and elicit the support of civic groups. The distribution of American popular movies abroad was linked to these CPI films. "Charlie Chaplin and Mary Pickford led *Pershing's Crusaders* and *America's Answer* into the enemy's territory," Creel once bragged, "and smashed another Hindenburg line."

Chaplin Som Greve
(Chaplin as Count)

Charlie Chaplin | 1889–1977

Sven Brasch (1886–1970)
Color linocut poster, 1918
87 x 63.2 cm (34 1/4 x 24 7/8 in.)
National Portrait Gallery, Smithsonian Institution

The movie industry, growing out of vaudeville and theatrical traditions that had always used poster advertising, adopted this medium as its primary form of promotion. Charlie Chaplin, one of the most versatile and talented figures of the early film industry, was a successful actor, writer, director, and producer. His screen image—the harassed but gallant Little Tramp who rarely lost his grip on his dignity, his derby, or his cane—had universal appeal. Chaplin's tragicomic persona disguised an astute businessman and a perfectionist filmmaker who is still respected for such classics as *Modern Times* (1936) and *The Great Dictator* (1940). By World War I, Chaplin had already gained international fame for the antics of his Tramp, as indicated in this poster by Danish artist Sven Brasch. Images such as this one transcended language barriers and kept audiences returning for the next Chaplin film.

WORLD
CIRKUS

CINEMA
VARIÉTÉ

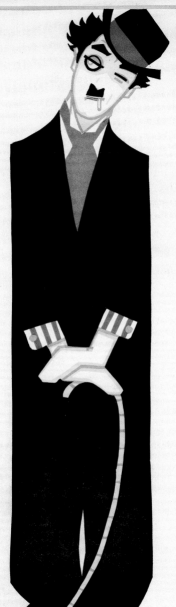

23.-31. December
hver Aften Kl. 7½:

CHAPLIN
SOM GREVE

Komisk Farce i 2 Akter

Variété-Afdeling:
Johnsen & Johnsen
Komisk Jonglør
Kay Whitt
International excentrick

Verdensspejlet
i Film

HANS
ÆGTESKAB

SKUESPIL I 5 AKTER
MED
NORMA TALMADGE
i Hovedrollen

Hver Søndag Eftm. Kl. 4:
Folkeforestilling
Smaa Priser

Skaaret i Linoleum efter Tegning af Sven Brasch

Akt. L. Ihrich, København.

Djaevlestenen (The Devil's Stone)
Geraldine Farrar | 1882–1967

Sven Brasch (1886–1970)
Color linocut poster, 1919
86 x 63.5 cm (33 7/8 x 25 in.)
National Portrait Gallery, Smithsonian Institution

In 1915, when director Cecil B. De Mille lured renowned opera star Geraldine Farrar to Hollywood, he hoped that her aura of high culture would add to the prestige of motion pictures. The beloved diva had no need of further accolades. Already popular in Europe, she was the reigning soprano at the Metropolitan Opera at the time, often paired with Enrico Caruso. Her sound recordings reached a mass audience. But Farrar, who considered herself as much an actress as a singer, ultimately appeared in fourteen silent films. According to Agnes de Mille, she was one of the first great international stars to try the "western [film] experiment." In *The Devil's Stone* (1917), Farrar's character is a "fishermaid" who becomes a modern urban wife. Sven Brasch's Danish poster, however, exploits the emerald of the title to depict Farrar as the glamorous leading lady that audiences expected, with evening gloves, jeweled diadem, and gown.

Blixtens Broder
(Brother of the Lightning)

William S. Hart | 1865–1946

Gunnar Håkansson (1891–1968)
Color lithographic poster, 1922
90.5 x 57.2 cm (35 5/8 x 22 1/2 in.)
National Portrait Gallery, Smithsonian Institution

Film actor William S. Hart was the first internationally renowned star of the American western. During his childhood in Minnesota, South Dakota, Kansas, and Iowa, he grew up around Sioux children, learned to speak Lakota, and eventually worked on cattle ranches. Hart trained as a stage actor but turned in the mid-1910s to the western film genre, introducing a new, gritty reality to settings, cast, and costumes. A writer, director, and screenwriter as well as a compelling screen presence, he became one of the most successful leading men of the era. By the 1920s, Hart's popularity in America was fading. But the lean, gun-toting cowboy—complete with bandana, boots, and buckskins—in this Swedish poster for the film originally titled *O'Malley of the Mounted*, promised to deliver what European audiences expected from Hart: a moralistic frontier drama spiced with bucking broncos and "the wild games of the cattle lands."

Douglas Fairbanks as the Gaucho
Douglas Fairbanks Sr. | 1883–1939

Ullman Manufacturing Company (active c. 1888–1946)
Color lithographic poster, 1927
47.1 x 62.1 cm (18 9/16 x 24 7/16 in.)
National Portrait Gallery, Smithsonian Institution

By 1927, when Douglas Fairbanks appeared as an Argentine cowboy outlaw in *The Gaucho,* he was world-renowned for the gusto and breezy athleticism he brought to his films. "There is, after all," one newspaper commented, "no one quite like him in the picture world." *The Gaucho* introduced new dramatic dimensions: an exotic South American setting, a bolas (a weighted, lariat-like weapon), and a spiritual angle inspired by Fairbanks's visit to the shrine of Our Lady of Lourdes. But the poster campaign marketed the forty-four-year-old actor as the swashbuckling adventurer audiences loved. His handsome, grinning face dominates the image, with the Andes and a bolas-wielding cowboy silhouetted below. The prominent cigarette is undoubtedly meant to imply the gaucho's raffish lawlessness before he encounters the healing miracles of a shrine. But given Fairbanks's popularity, it undoubtedly encouraged the growing glamour of smoking in public.

Colleen Moore in Lilac Time
Colleen Moore | 1902–1988

Batiste Madalena (1902–1989)
Hand-painted gouache poster with graphite, 1928
58.4 x 48 cm (23 x 18 7/8 in.)
National Portrait Gallery, Smithsonian Institution

George Eastman opened his elegant Rochester, New York, movie palace in 1922, hoping to upgrade the image of motion pictures (for which his company was producing the sprocketed film) as well as capitalize on their growing popularity. Most film exhibitors received a package of advertising "paper" from the studio, including small lobby and window cards, and posters in several sizes. Mass-produced advertising was not good enough for Eastman, however, who had ornate brass display cases designed for the exterior of his theater and hired a young Italian-born artist, Batiste Madalena, to paint original advertising signs. In his hand-painted poster for *Lilac Time,* Madalena focused on crisp art deco lettering and geometrical styling, diving airplanes, and Colleen Moore's classic flapper look, even though she plays a curly haired French country girl to Gary Cooper's World War I aviator.

BUSTER KEATON

L'OPÉRATEUR

FILM Metro-Goldwyn-Mayer

Buster Keaton L'Opérateur (The Cameraman)
Buster Keaton | 1895–1966

Jean-Albert Mercier (1899–1995)
Color lithographic poster, c. 1928
145.9 x 105.9 cm (57 7/16 x 41 11/16 in.)
National Portrait Gallery, Smithsonian Institution

Film comedian Buster Keaton is both behind the camera and in the spotlight in this image, made by French poster designer Jean-Albert Mercier at a time when Keaton claimed his silent movies actually did a bigger business in Europe than in America. This poster for Keaton's movie *The Cameraman* attracts attention with brilliant colors and clever geometric stylization of forms. But it also advertises the latest film by incorporating two of the actor's trademarks: the deadpan, expressionless face and a lively chase scene pitting the agile human figure against relentless mechanical forces. The latter is suggested by a circle of sketches expressing speed and motion in a never-ending contest. In Keaton's movies, James Agee wrote in his 1949 appraisal of silent film comics, "it seems that the whole universe is in exquisite flying motion and the one point of repose is [Keaton's] effortless, uninterested face."

Smash All Records

James Harold Doolittle | 1896–1993

James G. Haizlip | 1896–1983

Buehler (active c. 1932) for Edwards & Deutsch Lithography Company
Color lithographic poster with halftone, 1932
87.2 x 151.2 cm (34 5/16 x 59 1/2 in.)
National Portrait Gallery, Smithsonian Institution

When Jimmy Doolittle was featured on this 1932 Shell Oil Company advertisement, his achievements as a Massachusetts Institute of Technology–trained aeronautical engineer doing pioneer aviation research was eclipsed by his fame as a record-setting, trophy-winning stunt flyer about to compete in another race. The image is dated September 6, 1932, the day Doolittle won the one-hundred-mile Thompson Trophy race in Cleveland, and it also acknowledges another Shell flyer, Jimmy Haizlip, who had recently broken a transcontinental speed record. The poster, however, is designed to promote the Shell Oil Company and its products, not a specific event. The photographs of the two popular aviators are given a sense of immediacy in the context of a newspaper "extra," tipped up slightly so that the small headline, "All Major Events Won By Shell," is clearly legible.

Dr. Jekyll/Mr. Hyde
Fredric March | 1897–1975

Georg (active 1925–1949)
Color lithographic poster, c. 1932
99.2 x 68 cm (39 1/16 x 26 3/4 in.)
National Portrait Gallery, Smithsonian Institution

The on-camera morphing of Fredric March's handsome face into his monstrous alter ego in the 1931 film *Dr. Jekyll and Mr. Hyde* was a technical innovation accomplished with "expert cunning," according to one reviewer, through a series of gradual exposures. The Swedish poster for the film juxtaposes March's two faces, and the contrast is sharpened by red and black colors and stylish geometric lettering. Audiences were already familiar with Robert Louis Stevenson's chilling tale; the 1886 story had been adapted into a popular stage play and several silent film versions, including one starring John Barrymore. But director Rouben Mamoulian introduced a self-consciously Freudian notion of the duality of good and evil: "We are treating Hyde as the 'bad half' of Dr. Jekyll," he noted; "a separate personality, but not a separate person." March won an Academy Award for his expert impersonation of those contrasting selves.

Greta Garbo in Königin Christine (Greta Garbo in Queen Christina)

Greta Garbo | 1905–1990

A. M. Cay (lifedates unknown)
Color lithographic poster, 1934
144.8 x 97.5 cm (57 x 38 3/8 in.)
National Portrait Gallery, Smithsonian Institution

Portraiture—from film stills to carefully crafted glamour shots by Hollywood photographers—was a principal form of publicity for the intensely private actress Greta Garbo. Since she refused interviews and public appearances, the studio released a steady stream of images for her many fans. Garbo's famous face and proud pose confront the viewer directly in this German poster for her 1933 film *Queen Christina.* She had readily agreed to star in a fictionalized account of the independent-minded seventeenth-century Swedish queen, who occasionally dressed like a man and ultimately abdicated her throne for greater religious, intellectual, and personal freedom. In the film, director Rouben Mamoulian used the beauty and mystery of Garbo's face in his final shot of Queen Christina standing at the prow of a ship, silently contemplating her future. Some writers likened her "breathtaking and mystical expression" to the Mona Lisa.

HIT FAST!

HIT HARD!

W. F. HALSEY
ADMIRAL·U.S.NAVY

HIT OFTEN!

Produce for Your Navy

VICTORY BEGINS AT HOME !

Victory Begins at Home
Admiral William F. Halsey Jr. | 1882–1959

Unidentified artist for Industrial Incentive Division, Navy Department
Color photolithographic poster with halftone, c. 1940
101.7 x 76.1 cm (40 1/16 x 29 15/16 in.)
National Portrait Gallery, Smithsonian Institution;
gift of Leslie, Judith, and Gabri Schreyer and Alice Schreyer Batko

Although World War II posters frequently
depicted an average soldier, worker, or housewife,
some featured renowned personalities like Fleet
Admiral William F. Halsey, whose famous motto,
"Hit hard! Hit fast! Hit often!" seemed to embody
his commanding persona. This poster captures
the gusto of "Bull" Halsey, who was the first to
lead U.S. counterstrikes against Japan and won
victories in the Solomon Islands, the Philippines,
Okinawa, and other areas in the South Pacific.
Leaning forward, Halsey squints into the distance
with binoculars in hand as though he is in the
midst of attacking his enemy. Printed in the
millions for display in U.S. factories, industrial
incentive posters such as these conflated battle
lines with production lines, in this case seeming
to unite them under Halsey's command. Urging
industrial workers to join the fight, the poster
argues that what they are really "producing" is
victory at sea.

Yankee Doodle Dandy

James Cagney | 1904–1986

Continental Lithography Corporation (active c. 1925–57)
Color photolithographic halftone poster, 1942
195.2 x 197.7 cm (76 7/8 x 77 13/16 in.)
National Portrait Gallery, Smithsonian Institution

"Every time I see him work," Will Rogers said of James Cagney, "it looks to me like a bunch of firecrackers going off all at once." The 1942 movie *Yankee Doodle Dandy* channeled Cagney's legendary energy and brusque charm into the depiction of beloved songwriter-showman George M. Cohan. Cohan, who wrote such American classics as "Yankee Doodle Boy" and "Born on the Fourth of July," was the perfect subject for a patriotic wartime tribute. With stars and stripes, Cagney's well-known face, and the implicit reminder of Cohan's familiar songs, the poster was as heart-stirring as the flags and bunting of a war bond rally, while the high-kicking chorus girls promised a bit more fun. As its size suggests, outdoor advertising grew larger to attract the attention of increasingly faster automobile traffic; eventually the industry standardized the dimensions of the twenty-four-sheet billboard to facilitate national advertising.

Pvt. Joe Louis says...

"We're going to do our part ...and we'll win because we're on God's side"

For additional copies write to Graphics Division, Office of Facts and Figures, Washington, D. C. . . . Specify GPO Jacket No. 460469.

U. S. GOVERNMENT PRINTING OFFICE : 1942—O

Pvt. Joe Louis Says—
Joe Louis | 1914–1981

Unidentified artist for Graphics Division,
Office of Facts and Figures
Color photolithographic poster with halftone, 1942
101.5 x 72.3 cm (39 15/16 x 28 7/16 in.)
National Portrait Gallery, Smithsonian Institution

Heavyweight champion Joe Louis was so popular in the 1930s, according to reporter Earl Brown, that "his huge picture in fighting togs" adorned many African American community gathering spots. Different fighting togs but the same popular appeal made for an extremely effective government war poster, utilizing only the dramatically posed figure, an inspirational quote, and a vivid blue background. The poster does not attempt to recruit troops, sell war bonds, or encourage hard work in the factories. It is a general message to fellow black Americans to "do our part." Louis himself, who had turned down a commission when he enlisted in the army, helped to integrate athletic programs, boxed in exhibition matches to entertain the troops, and helped to raise money for military relief funds. At the end of the war, the army commended him for "exceptionally meritorious service."

"Above and Beyond the Call of Duty"
Dorie Miller | 1919–1943

David Stone Martin (1913–1992)
Color photolithographic poster with halftone, 1943
71.2 x 51.4 cm (28 1/16 x 20 1/4 in.)
National Portrait Gallery, Smithsonian Institution

This poster, designed by an Office of War Information art director, David Stone Martin, was one of several inspirational posters aimed at the black community. At the outbreak of World War II, the armed services practiced rigid discrimination against African Americans that included a stubborn reluctance to acknowledge black capabilities. When Japan attacked Pearl Harbor on December 7, 1941, navy messman Dorie Miller was serving on the USS *West Virginia*. Before abandoning ship, he braved enemy fire to carry a wounded officer to safety and, although not trained for combat, manned an antiaircraft gun, possibly downing at least one enemy plane. He eventually received a Navy Cross, but only after intense pressure by the black press. The poster's heroic overtones and quote gain extra poignancy in hindsight: Miller, later a messman on the USS *Liscombe Bay,* was killed when the aircraft carrier sank in the Pacific in November 1943.

"above and beyond the call of duty"

David Stone Martin

DORIE MILLER
Received the Navy Cross
at Pearl Harbor, May 27, 1942

OWI Poster No. 68.   Additional copies may be obtained upon request from the Division of Public Inquiries, Office of War Information, Washington, D. C.

U. S. GOVERNMENT PRINTING OFFICE : 1943—O-530629

A MOVIE IN TECHNICOLOR "COMBAT AMERICA"

PRODUCED AND NARRATED BY
MAJOR CLARK GABLE
FOR THE U. S. ARMY AIR FORCES

BUY EXTRA WAR BONDS

"Combat America"
Clark Gable | 1901–1960

Unidentified artist for the U.S. Treasury Department
Color photolithographic poster with halftone, 1944
81.6 x 61 cm (32 1/8 x 24 in.)
National Portrait Gallery, Smithsonian Institution;
gift of Beverly Jones Cox

U.S. Treasury Department posters often featured prominent faces to promote war bond drives. In 1942, devastated by the death of his wife Carole Lombard in a plane crash, film star Clark Gable joined the U.S. Army Air Force. Attached to a heavy bombardment group and assigned to procure footage for recruitment films, Gable flew on numerous bombing missions, with such a tolerance for risk that some considered it a death wish. After six months, having earned a Distinguished Flying Cross and other honors, he was sent home along with his crew. Their extensive combat footage resulted in four short films and one major feature, *Combat America,* which was used for training and shown in clubs and factories during the war. Although Gable was determined to do more than entertain, he understood the value of using his famous face to support the war effort at home.

I Want <u>You</u> / F. D. R.
Franklin D. Roosevelt | 1882–1945

James Montgomery Flagg (1877–1960)
Color photolithographic poster with halftone, 1944
53.9 x 42.3 cm (21 1/4 x 16 5/8 in.)
National Portrait Gallery, Smithsonian Institution

When James Montgomery Flagg drew his famous World War I "I Want You" recruiting poster, he turned to the mirror for his craggy image of Uncle Sam. Although inspired by the British image of a pointing Lord Kitchener, Flagg's version captured the public's imagination with special effectiveness. Along with the stern features of the self-portrait, the foreshortened hand gesture forged a personal connection with the viewer. A generation later, Flagg translated that familiar image into this presidential campaign piece promoting Franklin D. Roosevelt's unprecedented fourth term. The poster coyly avoids asking for votes, suggesting instead that America's duty was to convince the incumbent to run in order to "finish the job." The poster was issued by the Independent Voters' Committee of the Arts and Sciences for Roosevelt, founded in 1944 to promote a fourth term with the expectation that the president could deliver both victory and a progressive peace settlement.

WOODBURY

MATCHED MAKE-UP

*POWDER * ROUGE * LIPSTICK * OF THE STARS *

Veronica Lake

GLAMOROUS PARAMOUNT STAR

Woodbury Matched Make-Up
Veronica Lake | 1919–1973

Unidentified artist
Color photolithographic halftone poster stand-up, c. 1945
108 x 75.9 cm (42 1/2 x 29 7/8 in.)
National Portrait Gallery, Smithsonian Institution

The Woodbury Soap Company's innovative 1911 slogan "A skin you love to touch" focused on the consumer, not the product, and introduced sexual undertones to enhance the appeal of a basic face soap. In this 1940s "stand-up" poster for a drugstore window, Woodbury, still marketing with sex appeal, chose the actress Veronica Lake to promote its makeup. A successful leading lady for Paramount, Lake was one of Hollywood's darlings at the time. She was already a trendsetter; her blonde "peekaboo" hairstyle had launched a fashion craze for eye-covering curls. Here, in order to focus attention on her complexion, there is only a hint of an errant wave. With soft, peach-colored petals in the background to match the actress's exquisite face, and with Lake's plunging black tulle neckline, the ad promises the Woodbury consumer not only delicate femininity but also a touch of naughty Hollywood glamour.

A Good Man Is Hard to Find

Harry S. Truman | 1884–1972

Thomas Dewey | 1902–1971

Ben Shahn (1898–1969)
Color lithographic poster, 1948
115.7 x 75.7 cm (45 9/16 x 29 13/16 in.)
National Portrait Gallery, Smithsonian Institution

Although the person is the product in most
political posters, candidate Henry A. Wallace does
not appear in Ben Shahn's 1948 poster for the
Progressive Party. Instead, the poster focuses on
creating negative, satirical images of Democrat
Harry Truman and Republican Thomas Dewey.
It was based on a much-publicized photograph
of Vice President Truman playing a piano with
actress Lauren Bacall lounging seductively on
top. Substituting Dewey for Bacall, Shahn cast the
political skills of both presidential candidates in
a frivolous light, emphasizing the message that
"A Good Man Is Hard to Find" in the two major
parties. Shahn first produced a painting that
served as the backdrop for Wallace's appearance
at the Progressive Party's convention in July 1948.
It was reproduced in the form of this beautifully
printed lithographic poster and distributed
nationwide, along with postcards of the image.

Quarto Potere (The Fourth Estate)
Orson Welles | 1915–1985

Unidentified artist
Color photolithographic halftone poster, 1948
199.5 x 142 cm (78 9/16 x 55 7/8 in.)
National Portrait Gallery, Smithsonian Institution

The post–World War II Italian posters of American films often translated well-known film stills into dramatic painted advertisements. This poster features the image of Orson Welles playing a powerful publishing tycoon in the movie *Citizen Kane*. (The Italian title translates to *The Fourth Estate*.) Star, director, producer, and one of the writers of the screenplay, Welles is closely identified with the cinematic innovations that *Citizen Kane* introduced. Critics recognized the film's excellence at the time of its release, and it earned an Oscar for Best Original Screenplay in 1941. But newspaper magnate William Randolph Hearst felt it was a personal attack and refused to run positive reviews in his papers, which helped to delay *Citizen Kane's* commercial success. The poster focuses on a photographic still of Welles's Kane campaigning for governor. An added background cityscape and dramatically lit crowd of listeners heighten the appeal.

Notorious!

Alfred Hitchcock | 1899–1980
Cary Grant | 1904–1986
Ingrid Bergman | 1915–1982
Claude Rains | 1889–1967

Morini (lifedates unknown)
Color photolithographic poster with halftone, c. 1950
202.6 x 145.4 cm (79 3/4 x 57 1/4 in.)
National Portrait Gallery, Smithsonian Institution

As banned American films finally arrived in Italy after World War II, the revived Italian poster industry turned out spectacular advertising, such as this image for the 1946 spy thriller *Notorious.* Director Alfred Hitchcock had paired for the first time two of his favorite actors of the 1940s, Cary Grant and Ingrid Bergman. In the film, which was both a popular and critical success in America, Hitchcock exposed the darker side of Grant's personality, focusing more on psychological tensions than on action scenes to further the suspense. The poster, however, features the love triangle between Grant, Bergman, and Claude Rains, who had won an Academy Award nomination for his depiction of a pro-Nazi spy. Especially effective in this poster is the unusual addition of Hitchcock himself, depicted here in a controlling, puppeteer-like pose.

IL CAPOLAVORO DI ALFRED HITCHCOCK
CARY GRANT
INGRID BERGMAN
CLAUDE
RAINS
LOUIS
CALHERN
UN FILM DI ALFRED
HITCHCOCK
MORINI
NOTORIOUS!
(L'AMANTE PERDUTA)
SCENEGGIATURA DI BEN HECHT
UNA PRODUZIONE DI DAVID O. SELZNICK

Trinidad

Rita Hayworth | 1918–1987
Glenn Ford | 1916–2006

Anselmo Ballester (1897–1974)
Color photolithographic halftone poster, 1953
197.9 x 140.2 cm (77 15/16 x 55 3/16 in.)
National Portrait Gallery, Smithsonian Institution

In this poster for the film *Affair in Trinidad,* the artist focused on Columbia Pictures's carefully constructed image for its leading lady, Rita Hayworth. Born Margarita Carmen Cansino, the daughter and onetime partner of a Spanish dancer, Hayworth was transformed by the early 1940s into a redheaded film goddess. In this Italian movie poster, the sensuality and vitality of her brilliantly colored figure is in marked contrast to the monochromatic depiction of costar Glenn Ford, with his grim gesture of violence. Because of the lack of interaction between them, each portrayal suggests an iconic pose rather than a specific scene. Veteran poster artist Anselmo Ballester cared more about capturing a mood than conveying specific details of the film, and in fact the images come from a previous Hayworth-Ford film, *Gilda.* "I must suggest," Ballester once noted; "the rest is up to the movie."

Fronte del Porto (On the Waterfront)

Marlon Brando | 1924–2004

Anselmo Ballester (1897–1974)
Color photolithographic halftone poster, 1954
187 x 128 cm (73 5/8 x 50 3/8 in.)
National Portrait Gallery, Smithsonian Institution

Director Elia Kazan's 1954 film *On the Waterfront,* depicting the gritty life of mob-ruled longshoremen, was nominated for twelve Academy Awards and won eight, including a Best Actor Oscar for Marlon Brando. In this Italian poster, designer Anselmo Ballester placed a terrifying baling hook in the foreground and added blood, a gun, and a looming mob to suggest the violent melodrama of the picture. The striding figure of Brando as ex-boxer Terry Malloy conveys more than just the film's story line. At nearly life size, it also expressed the actor's powerful physical intensity, grace, and sexual magnetism. In his early films, Brando "strode through American popular culture like lightning on legs," one critic wrote. His "method" approach to acting influenced many, and the electric presence he brought to his troubled characters projected an attitude—conflicted and vulnerable—that spoke to the disaffected youth of the postwar period.

BALLESTER
COLUMBIA PICTURES presenta:
MARLON
BRANDO
in
FRONTE del PORTO
UNA PRODUZIONE DI
ELIA KAZAN
con KARL MALDEN - LEE J. COBB
ROD STEIGER - PAT HENNING e EVA MARIE SAINT
COLUMBIA
CEIAD
PRODOTTO DA SAM SPIEGEL - SOGGETTO DI BUDD SCHULBERG - MUSICA DI LEONARD BERNSTEIN - REGIA DI ELIA KAZAN

Niagara
Marilyn Monroe | 1926–1962

Unidentified artist
Color photolithographic poster with halftone, 1953
104.5 x 68.5 cm (41 1/8 x 26 15/16 in.)
National Portrait Gallery, Smithsonian Institution;
gift of John P. Banning Jr.

American film posters of the 1950s were generally unambitious assemblages of film stills. But this memorable poster for 20th Century-Fox's 1953 film *Niagara,* which merges a curvaceous Marilyn Monroe into the roaring torrent of water, blasts its sexual content with candor and not a little humor. In *Niagara,* Monroe plays an adulterous wife scheming to murder her depressed war-veteran husband. Although not written as a starring vehicle for her, she dominated the film. The poster's inset photo hints at her sensuous appeal and her ability to project a naïve vulnerability into her character as she underestimates her violent husband. *Niagara* launched Monroe as a major actress and, as the poster suggests, also created a winning formula for marketing her. With its lurid text and romance novel illustration, the poster successfully promotes her sex appeal to the extent of discounting any acting talent.

Carmen Jones

Dorothy Dandridge | 1922–1965

Unidentified artist
Color photolithographic poster with halftone, 1954
195.4 x 104.9 cm (76 15/16 x 41 5/16 in.)
National Portrait Gallery, Smithsonian Institution

Film poster advertising after World War II generally retained the photographic realism and unambitious designs of wartime messages. This poster, however, advertising Otto Preminger's *Carmen Jones,* an updated version of Bizet's famous opera, stands out as an unusually successful example from the time period. The beautiful Dorothy Dandridge was hailed by critics in this role. She became the first African American to win a Best Actress Oscar nomination and the first black woman to appear on the cover of *Life* magazine (wearing the same black and red outfit). Unfortunately, what seemed to be the beginning of a stellar career was actually its climax, since good roles for black actresses were practically nonexistent in mainstream films. But every element of the poster for *Carmen Jones*— vivacious pose, life-size scale, ambiguous space, simplified color scheme, and jazzy lettering— adds to her glamour and promise.

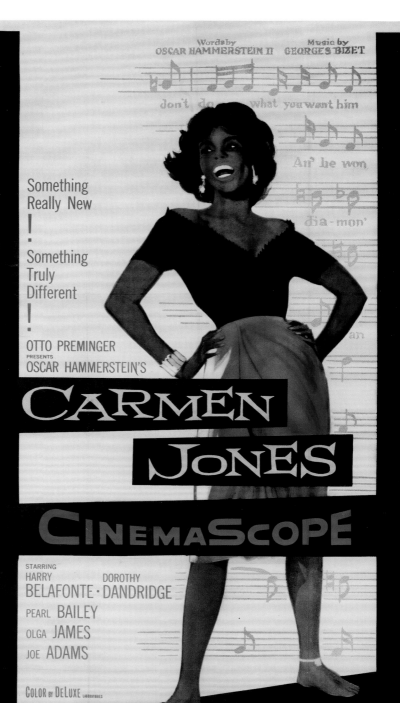

GOLDWATER

FOR PRESIDENT

 VOTE ROW A–ALL THE WAY

Goldwater for President
Barry Goldwater | 1909–1998

Amalgamated Lithographers
(active 1882–present) for Tenny Press
Color photolithographic halftone poster, 1964
137.5 x 101.7 cm (54 1/8 x 40 1/16 in.)
National Portrait Gallery, Smithsonian Institution

"Extremism in the defense of liberty is no vice, and . . . moderation in the pursuit of justice is no virtue," declared Arizona Senator Barry Goldwater when he accepted the Republican Party's nomination for president in 1964. Although the Republican ticket was defeated by incumbent Lyndon Baines Johnson, Goldwater's campaign helped set the stage for the rise of the conservative movement in late twentieth-century America and demonstrate its strength in the South and the West. This election poster, enhanced only by its large scale and bold "gold" border, is a straightforward presentation of face, name, and voting instructions. It was based on Goldwater's official campaign photograph, which pictured him with skewed glasses, an appealing touch of imperfection. A similarly bordered format was used for the companion poster depicting his running mate, New York congressman William E. Miller.

Count Basie and Band/
Stan Getz and Quartet

Count Basie | 1904–1984

Stan Getz | 1927–1991

Seymour Chwast (born 1931)
Color photolithographic poster, 1963
93.3 x 47.9 cm (36 3/4 x 18 7/8 in.)
National Portrait Gallery, Smithsonian Institution;
gift of Jack Rennert

"Polish was the keynote of a jazz concert by the Stan Getz Quartet and Count Basie's orchestra," a *New York Times* reviewer wrote on November 28, 1963, noticing that Getz imbued even the gentlest phrases with "a sinew and mettle that keep them alive and vigorous." Seymour Chwast's innovative poster, echoing the vitality and assurance of the renowned jazz musicians, advertised the concert with cartoonish figures, green skin tones, and a blue horn. Chwast, along with Milton Glaser and other graphic artists, founded Push Pin Studios in 1954. Despite different styles, they all sought an integration of illustration, design, and typography, and were attracted, as Glaser noted, to things "orthodox modernism" despised, including ornamentation and hand-drawn pictures. Going against the grain of photographic magazine illustration and minimalist abbreviation in corporate advertising, Push Pin Studios introduced a fresh and influential approach to poster art and graphic design.

K & F Productions presents

Chwast

COUNT
Basie **Getz** STAN
AND BAND AND QUARTET

&   Jimmy Rushing

Nov. 27, 8:30 pm
Lincoln Center
Philharmonic Hall
TICKETS: $5.50 5.00 4.50 4.00 3.50
On sale now at Lincoln Center. Mail orders: K & F Productions 235 East 54 St.

Dylan
Bob Dylan | born 1941

Milton Glaser (born 1929)
Color photolithographic poster with halftone, 1966
83.8 x 55.8 cm (33 x 21 15/16 in.)
National Portrait Gallery, Smithsonian Institution

Milton Glaser, one of the founders of New York's Push Pin Studios, created an icon of 1960s counterculture in his now-classic *Dylan* poster. It was a new form of poster, according to the artist, created as a bonus insert for the *Bob Dylan's Greatest Hits* album of 1967. Dylan, who wrote such songs as "Blowin' in the Wind" and "Mr. Tambourine Man," was the folk-rock poet of the 1960s, and Glaser used his famous name as a typographically innovative design feature on the poster. In addition, by pairing a bold, black profile inspired by Marcel Duchamp's self-portrait silhouette with bright-colored writhing curves reminiscent of psychedelic rock posters, Glaser merged West Coast exuberance with pared-down East Coast stylization. According to some reports, six million copies were distributed, and the *Dylan* poster has been spotted in such remote areas as a hut in the Amazon rain forest.

Junior Wells

Junior Wells | born 1934

Victor Moscoso (born 1936)
Color photolithographic poster, 1966
51 x 36 cm (20 1/16 x 14 3/16 in.)
National Portrait Gallery, Smithsonian Institution

The psychedelic posters emanating out of San Francisco in the mid-1960s became the visual symbol of the counterculture for youth across the country. Rock impresario Bill Graham capitalized on these new styles for events he organized for San Francisco's Fillmore West Auditorium. Victor Moscoso produced this Fillmore poster advertising popular blues performer Junior Wells in 1966. One of the few poster designers with academic art training—he had studied at the Cooper Union, Yale, and the San Francisco Art Institute—Moscoso generally found his art school background of little help in experimenting with poster styles. But some of his pioneering effects he credited in part to his color studies with Josef Albers at Yale. "Hot" colors in wild combinations, Moscoso realized, could "load up the surface" of his poster, creating an intensity that made the image vibrate optically.

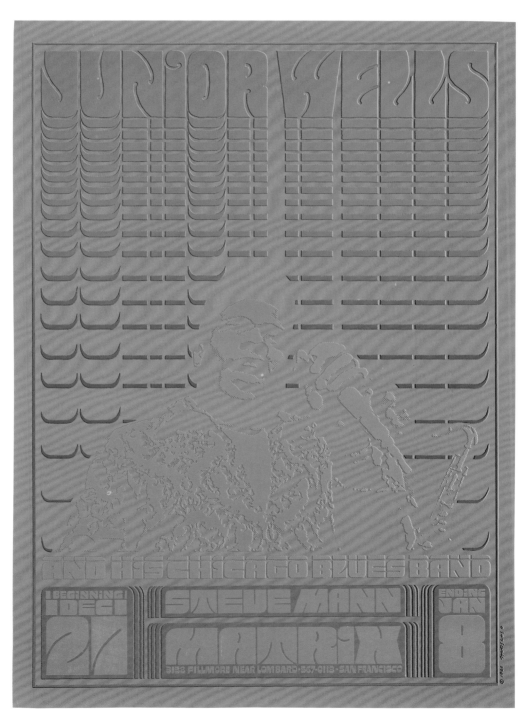

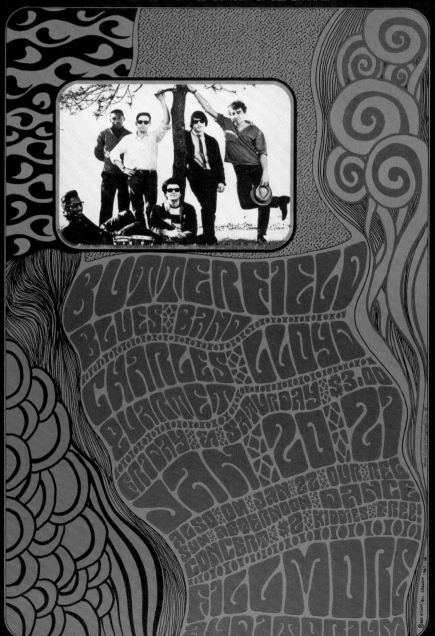

Butterfield Blues Band

Robert Wesley Wilson (born 1937)
Color photolithographic poster with halftone, 1967
55.5 x 37.4 cm (21 7/8 x 14 3/4 in.)
National Portrait Gallery, Smithsonian Institution;
gift of Jack Banning

Wes Wilson, who designed Bill Graham's first Fillmore Auditorium ads, was "probably the most influential designer of hippie posters," according to *Graphis* magazine in 1968. In this poster, he embedded a photograph of the Butterfield Blues Band into a background of swirling shapes, unexpected colors, and odd lettering. Wilson recalled selecting his colors from hallucinatory experiences with LSD. His manipulation of words was particularly trendsetting. Wilson liked working freehand and filling up the space with ornament, so when he encountered a book of turn-of-the-century Viennese Secessionist posters, he adapted their sinuous lettering to his own art. "Playing with foreground and background," he noted, "helped me work out patterns and shapes." Much to Graham's frustration, Wilson's habit of burying pertinent information underneath "oozes and ebbs and flows and liquidy movement" often made his (and subsequent designers') posters illegible, but it did encourage viewers to stare longer.

Jefferson Airplane

Jim Blashfield (active c. 1967), after Herb Greene
Color photolithographic poster with halftone, 1967
52.3 x 35.2 cm (20 9/16 x 13 7/8 in.)
National Portrait Gallery, Smithsonian Institution;
gift of Leslie and Alice Schreyer

Rock promoter Bill Graham helped guide the Jefferson Airplane band to success in the vanguard of the country's anti-establishment hippie revolution. This advertisement for their 1967 concert at Graham's Fillmore Auditorium has all the elements of the classic psychedelic poster: searing colors, portraits of the musicians, ambiguous hand-drawn elements, and swelling letters that dance before the viewer's eyes. Such advertisements suggested the dizzying, multisensory experience of many Fillmore dance concerts, which were charged with high-decibel music, light shows, frenetic movement, and, often, mind-expanding drugs. The posters, visual symbols of the rock scene and the counterculture, began to vanish as soon as they appeared, grabbed by increasing numbers of collectors. Graham and other publishers produced extra quantities for retail sale, and poster stores opened in all the major cities. "Posters in every dimension and description . . . are being plastered across the U.S.," *Life* magazine reported in 1967.

BILL GRAHAM PRESENTS THE SAN FRANCISCO SCENE

JEFFERSON!! AIRPLANE

GRATEFUL DEAD

BIG BROTHER AND THE HOLDING CO.

LIGHT SHOW BY GLENN MCKAY HEAD LIGHTS

AT THE HOLLYWOOD BOWL

PRESENTED IN
CONJUNCTION
WITH
RADIO KRLA
TICKETS AT ALL
SOUTHLAND
AGENCIES
AND
HOLLYWOOD
BOWL
PHOTO BY HERB GREENE

JIM BLASHFIELD ©1967 by BILL GRAHAM #81

What becomes a Legend most?
Blackglama
BLACKGLAMA® IS THE WORLD'S FINEST NATURAL DARK RANCH MINK BRED ONLY IN AMERICA BY THE GREAT LAKES MINK MEN

What becomes a Legend most?
Bette Davis | 1908–1989

Richard Avedon (1923–2004) for Blackglama
Photolithographic halftone poster, 1968
70.3 x 55.2 cm (27 11/16 x 21 3/4 in.)
National Portrait Gallery, Smithsonian Institution

When the Great Lakes Mink Association asked
New York advertiser Jane Trahey to rehabilitate
the fur industry after a sharp decline in the 1960s,
she conceived the famous Blackglama advertising
campaign. Launched in 1968, the series of posters
paired Richard Avedon's photographs of such
mink-garbed celebrities as Bette Davis with the
tantalizing caption "What becomes a Legend
most?" No identifying name was necessary.
Within two years, Blackglama was the most
prestigious black ranch mink in the world, the
fur industry was thriving, and stars clamored
to become a "legend" and take home a mink coat.
Bette Davis was in the initial series of posters.
The agency representative remembered her
nonstop smoking in the car en route to Avedon's
studio. But she was a pro. "Ten cigarettes later," he
recalled, "we had captured the legend."

What becomes a Legend most?
Judy Garland | 1922–1969

Richard Avedon (1923–2004) for Blackglama
Photolithographic halftone poster, 1968
70.3 x 55.2 cm (27 11/16 x 21 3/4 in.)
National Portrait Gallery, Smithsonian Institution

Advertising agency associate Peter Rogers had the job of escorting the stars as they came into town for their Blackglama photo shoots. "Managing" Judy Garland turned out to be a challenge. She had stayed up most of the previous night, joining Tony Bennett at his performance at the Waldorf and visiting with him afterward. When Rogers called for Garland the next morning to take her to Avedon's studio, the hotel room was a disaster, littered with empty vodka bottles and feathers from a pillow fight with a friend. But Garland pulled herself together, and by the time her hair and makeup had been done, she "looked terrific." She sang along with one of her records and the photo session went well. Ultimately, however, they chose a non-performing shot: "somehow," Rogers remembered, "it seemed to capture the Garland image more poignantly."

What becomes a Legend most?

Blackglama

What becomes a Legend most?
Shirley MacLaine | born 1934

Bill King (1939–1987) for Blackglama
Photolithographic halftone poster, 1977
70.5 x 55.2 cm (27 3/4 x 21 3/4 in.)
National Portrait Gallery, Smithsonian Institution;
gift of Poster America

Celebrity photographer Bill King took over the successful Blackglama campaign from Richard Avedon in 1972. When he photographed Shirley MacLaine, King and agency associate Peter Rogers decided in advance that they wanted a dance shot. Although MacLaine worked hard for the camera, according to Rogers, the perfect image was not easy to capture, especially as the actress insisted on wearing white majorette boots for many of the pictures. But she liked the final picture—without the boots—and it became one of the most popular Blackglama posters.

The Blackglama campaign, exploiting a heady mix of glamour and commerce, continued to sell coats throughout the next couple of decades. After its successful example, advertisers realized the compelling allure of celebrity figures, and advertising campaigns using sports and entertainment stars to promote products proliferated.

Bring the Troops Home Now
Lyndon B. Johnson | 1908–1973

Nancy Coner (1930–1974)
Color photolithographic poster with halftone, c. 1966–68
57.1 x 44.5 cm (22 1/2 x 17 1/2 in.)
National Portrait Gallery, Smithsonian Institution;
gift of Leslie, Judith, and Gabri Schreyer
and Alice Schreyer Batko

The anti–Vietnam War movement became a
defining marker of youth culture in the late 1960s
and early 1970s as increasing numbers of students
realized the strength of their collective voice.
Posters were a frequently used tool of protest,
displayed on college campuses and held aloft
in marches and demonstrations. The Student
Mobilization Committee, a national organization
that encouraged the formation of campus
committees to end the war, issued the poster
Bring the Troops Home Now. The phrase was also
a slogan for antiwar organizations and rallies, as
well as the title of a newsletter that sought to
direct the movement toward troop reduction. The
poster's designer, Nancy Coner, summoned many
potent signals of the era, including rock-poster
lettering, a pinwheel, helmeted and slain troops,
riot police, a pontificating President Johnson, and
placards with more antiwar slogans.

ENGRAVED BY STEVEN MARTIN

"I DON'T KNOW WHAT WILL HAPPEN NOW. WE HAVE GOT DIF-
FICULT DAYS AHEAD, BUT IT DOESN'T MATTER WITH ME BE-
CAUSE I'VE BEEN TO THE MOUNTAIN TOP. LIKE ANYBODY ELSE
I WOULD LIKE TO LIVE A LONG LIFE. BUT IM NOT CONCERNED
WITH THAT. I JUST WANT TO DO GOD'S WILL AND HE HAS AL-
LOWED ME TO GO UP THE MOUNTAIN. I SEE THE PROM-
ISED LAND. I MAY NOT GET THERE WITH YOU, BUT I WANT YOU
TO KNOW TONIGHT THAT WE AS A PEOPLE WILL GET TO THE
PROMISED LAND. I AM HAPPY TONIGHT THAT I AM NOT WOR-
RIED ABOUT ANYTHING. I'M NOT FEARING ANY MAN. MINE
EYES HAVE SEEN THE GLORY OF THE COMING OF THE LORD."

Martin Luther King Jr.

"I don't know what will happen now"
Martin Luther King Jr. | 1929–1968

Stefan Martin (1936–1994), after Ben Shahn
Photolithographic poster after wood engraving, 1968
72.3 x 55.9 cm (28 7/16 x 22 in.)
National Portrait Gallery, Smithsonian Institution;
gift of Mary Hanes Holbeck

Shortly after Martin Luther King's death, the Southern Christian Leadership Conference used this poster—issued in an edition of one hundred—for a fundraising drive. The portrait was based on a drawing by Ben Shahn commissioned for *Time* magazine's March 19, 1965 cover. *Time*'s publisher noted that Shahn, "as famed in his own medium of protest as King is in his," greatly admired the civil rights leader and felt that King had "moved more people by his oratory" than anyone else. After the artist's friend Stefan Martin made a wood engraving based on the drawing, Shahn authorized its use in support of various causes. This 1968 poster included two additions to the portrait: the orange seal or artist's "chop" that Shahn had made in Japan incorporating the letters of the Hebrew alphabet, and an excerpt from King's famous "mountaintop" speech in the artist's own distinctive lettering.

Huey P. Newton, Minister of Defence
Huey Newton | 1942–1989

Unidentified artist
Photolithographic halftone poster, c. 1968
88.9 x 58.4 cm (35 x 23 in.)
National Portrait Gallery, Smithsonian Institution

When organizers of the Black Panther Party set up this scene for a photographer in 1967—enthroning the young "minister of defence" Huey Newton in a wicker chair and surrounding him with a spear, a gun, an animal pelt, and African shields—they hoped to produce a visual emblem of the movement for the second issue of their newspaper. But the photograph became a more potent and far-reaching symbol of radical protest than anyone could have guessed. It was published in the *New York Times,* the *Los Angeles Times,* and elsewhere. When Newton was wounded and arrested during a traffic-stop altercation and subsequently convicted of killing the policeman, supporters rallied to get him out of jail. The "Free Huey" movement, adopted by many on the radical left, got international exposure. Protestors carried this photographic poster during massive rallies and displayed it as a symbol of leftist political sympathies.

"The racist dog policemen must withdraw immediately from our communities, cease their wanton murder and brutality and torture of black people, or face the wrath of the armed people."

Huey P. Newton, Minister of Defence

Black Panther Party for Self Defence
P.O. Box 8641, Emeryville, California

Winner?

Janis Joplin | 1943–1970

Jimi Hendrix | 1942–1970

L & S Productions (active 1970s)
Color photolithographic halftone poster, 1970
92 x 36.1 cm (36 1/4 x 14 3/16 in.)
National Portrait Gallery, Smithsonian Institution

In a time when musicians were seen as leaders in a cultural revolution, this pill-shaped poster, highlighting the drug-related deaths of Jimi Hendrix and Janis Joplin at tragically young ages, questioned the lifestyle choices of such trendsetters. Hendrix shot to fame with his groundbreaking guitar playing. Joplin, a bluesy rock singer with a powerful voice, electrified audiences with her explosive performance style, delivered with unrestrained movement and a variety of wailing, whispering, and shrieking sounds. Their deaths in 1970 propelled the emerging anti-drug movement, which would eventually lead to President Richard Nixon declaring a war on drugs in 1971 and creating the Drug Enforcement Administration in 1973. The juxtaposition of these popular icons with the question "Winner?" summarizes the grip of the era's drug culture and the beginning of a concerted effort to curtail its power.

America Needs McGovern: He Can Put It Together

George McGovern | born 1922

Larry Rivers (1923–2002), after Malcolm Varon
Color photolithographic halftone poster, 1972
75.6 x 58.4 cm (29 3/4 x 23 in.)
National Portrait Gallery, Smithsonian Institution;
gift of Virginia Zabriskie

Cycling the viewer's eyes away from a crossed-out sketch of President Nixon to a smiling photograph of George McGovern, this poster by renowned artist Larry Rivers argued that America needed the 1972 Democratic presidential nominee to put the country's scattered pieces back together. Using a wide range of visual techniques, including pencil sketches, stencil, photography, collage, varied lettering, and puzzle pieces, the artist gave the poster the informal, youthful, and almost rebellious tone that characterized aspects of McGovern's presidential bid and famous campaign against the Vietnam War. The poster's "togetherness" theme reinforces the message behind the candidate's massive "Together for McGovern at the Garden" rally of 20,000 supporters in Madison Square Garden in 1972; many of the McGovern campaign posters echo the word.

America Needs

McGOVERN

HE CAN
PUT IT TOGETHER

Rivero 68/100

See Bette at the Palace December 3-22

AMSEL

Bette Midler
Bette Midler | born 1945

Richard Amsel (1947–1985)
Color photolithographic poster, 1973
114.3 x 74.9 cm (45 x 29 1/2 in.)
National Portrait Gallery, Smithsonian Institution;
gift of Jack Rennert

"She's 5'1" . . . absolutely dizzy, and rarer than a homemade honeybun" raved an awed reporter in 1972 about the singer-comedienne Bette Midler, then performing at New York City's Continental Baths. "Her hair is "red as a Pomegranate. . . . Her bosom is formidable. . . . She moves fiercely on tiny feet strapped into the highest platform wedgies since Carmen Miranda." Richard Amsel, an emerging talent who had recently won a nationwide contest to design the poster for *Hello, Dolly!,* caught her energy and flair in his 1973 poster. Midler's accompanist, Barry Manilow, who produced her first and second albums, admired Amsel's work, and Midler agreed he should design the cover and advertising art. His stylized strutting figure graced Midler's second album, promoted a national tour, and here announced her appearance to sold-out audiences at New York's Palace Theater in December 1973. A similar image was reused for later albums and tours.

We Are Still Here

Leonard Crow Dog | born 1942

Paul Davis (born 1938)
Color halftone poster, 1977
101.8 x 68.8 cm (40 1/16 x 27 1/16 in.)
National Portrait Gallery, Smithsonian Institution;
gift of Jack Rennert

Social equality became a rallying point for many political activists in the 1960s and 1970s as various movements supporting civil rights, women's liberation, migrant workers, homosexuals, and other marginalized groups sought to transform American life. Posters became not only symbols of active protest but dorm-room signals of affiliation with popular causes. The poster *We Are Still Here* featured Leonard Crow Dog, a charismatic leader of the American Indian Movement. As the poster's caption, "Medicine Man," suggests, Crow Dog redirected the movement to place greater emphasis on Native American traditions, rituals, and spiritual heritage. Push Pin Studio artist Paul Davis, who also made posters supporting Che Guevara and César Chávez, used a low viewpoint to give Crow Dog heroic dimensions. Davis's distinctive posters, with their simple, bold imagery, bright colors, and faux-naif distortions, seemed to speak to the age.

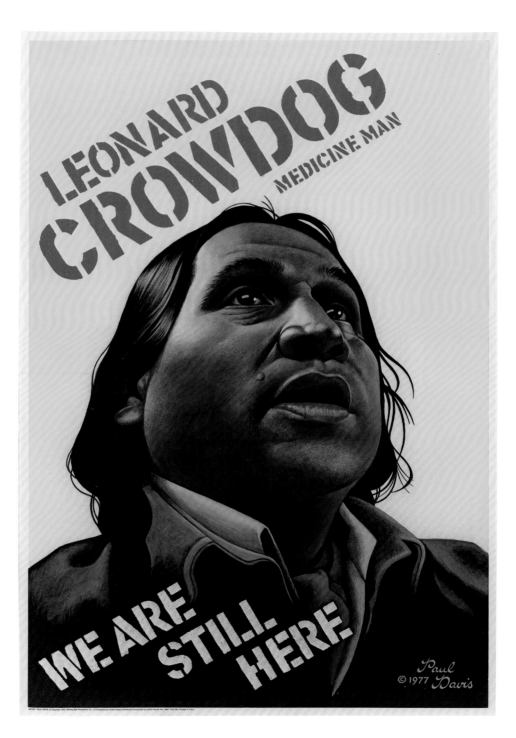

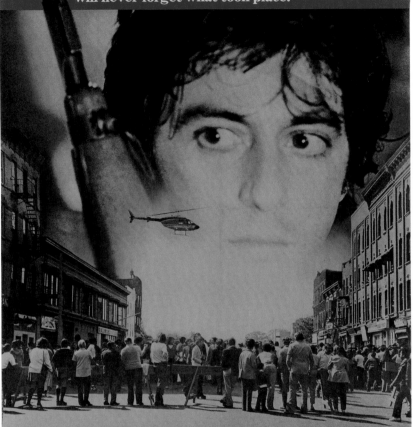

In August, 1972, Sonny Wortzik robbed a bank.
250 cops, the F.B.I., 8 hostages and 2,000 onlookers
will never forget what took place.

AL PACINO

An Artists Entertainment Complex, Inc. Production

DOG DAY AFTERNOON

Also Starring JOHN CAZALE · JAMES BRODERICK and CHARLES DURNING as Moretti
Produced by MARTIN BREGMAN and MARTIN ELFAND · Directed by SIDNEY LUMET
Screenplay by FRANK PIERSON · Film Editor DEDE ALLEN · TECHNICOLOR®
From WARNER BROS A WARNER COMMUNICATIONS COMPANY

Dog Day Afternoon
Al Pacino | born 1940

Unidentified artist
Color photolithographic poster with halftone, 1975
195.6 x 104.9 cm (77 x 41 5/16 in.)
National Portrait Gallery, Smithsonian Institution

In this poster for the 1975 crime drama *Dog Day Afternoon,* Al Pacino's likeness looms large over a gathered crowd of police officers, FBI agents, and other onlookers. Pacino did seem larger than life at the time. Portraying complex characters with a subtlety and intensity few others could match in such films as *The Godfather, Serpico,* and *The Godfather II,* he was the prototypic male star of the 1970s, bringing a sense of tough realism to his roles. *Dog Day Afternoon* was based on the story of a failed 1972 New York City bank robbery, which had captured media attention at the time. Pacino's performance as Sonny Wortzik, an unemployed Vietnam veteran, earned him his fourth Oscar nomination in consecutive years and the Best Actor award. His energetic portrayal of Sonny, critic Gene Siskel said, "made me believe the unbelievable."

Qualcuno Volo' Sul Nido del Cuculo (One Flew Over the Cuckoo's Nest)

Jack Nicholson | born 1937

Unidentified artist
Color photolithographic poster with halftone, c. 1975
198.8 x 139.5 cm (78 1/4 x 54 15/16 in.)
National Portrait Gallery, Smithsonian Institution;
acquired through the generosity of David C. Ward

The manic face of Jack Nicholson in an Italian poster for *One Flew Over the Cuckoo's Nest* encapsulated that wicked wink-and-grin personality that brought the actor cult status as the prototypic antihero of film. In the 1975 dramatization of Ken Kesey's best-selling novel, Nicholson played a minor offender who tried to outwit prison officials by pretending to need psychiatric care. The movie swept the Oscars, winning all of the major awards, including Nicholson's first for Best Actor. The counterculture appeal of this political allegory is captured by the vivid poster graphics. Showing Nicholson during a pivotal scene, the expanding boxes suggest the pulsating trauma of electrotherapy and the lobotomy used to quell his rebellion. The style alludes to minimal and pop art, including the Benday dots of Roy Lichtenstein, as well as to the pervasive influence of the Italian director Michelangelo Antonioni's *Blow-Up* of 1966.

JACK NICHOLSON

QUALCUNO VOLO' SUL NIDO DEL CUCULO

Fantasy Films PRESENTA

UN FILM DI MILOS FORMAN
JACK NICHOLSON IN QUALCUNO VOLO' SUL NIDO DEL CUCULO · CON LOUISE FLETCHER
E WILLIAM REDFIELD · SCENEGGIATURA DI LAWRENCE HAUBEN E BO GOLDMAN
DAL ROMANZO DI KEN KESEY · DIRETTORE DELLA FOTOGRAFIA HASKELL WEXLER
MUSICA DI JACK NITZSCHE · PRODOTTO DA SAUL ZAENTZ E MICHAEL DOUGLAS
REGIA DI MILOS FORMAN · COLORE · United Artists Europa Inc.

APOCALYPSE NOW   790143

Apocalypse Now

Marlon Brando | 1924–2004
Martin Sheen | born 1940

Unidentified artist
Color photolithographic halftone poster, 1979
104 x 68.6 cm (40 15/16 x 27 in.)
National Portrait Gallery, Smithsonian Institution;
gift of Saul Zalesch

By the time he was recruited for Francis Ford Coppola's 1979 *Apocalypse Now,* the influential but controversial actor Marlon Brando had become almost a parody of himself. Although he was paid generously for his relatively small role in this Vietnam-era war epic, he arrived for the shoot grossly overweight and ill-prepared. Nonetheless, Brando, playing Colonel Kurtz, a Special Forces officer driven mad by the moral ambiguity and unendurable horror of war, looms at the heart of the film in Coppola's vision, as this poster suggests. Brando shaved his head for the role, and his partially improvised monologue is filmed in a surreal, shadowy close-up. Despite the director's problems with Brando, Coppola conceded the importance of his role. The big scene of this adventure-action movie, he claimed, "is not another helicopter battle, but it's a guy, a face, alone in a dark room, telling the truth."

Labor's Centennial

Lane Kirkland | 1922–1999

Robert Rauschenberg | born 1925
Offset lithographic poster, 1981
91.4 x 61 cm (36 x 24 in.)
National Portrait Gallery, Smithsonian Institution;
gift of Irena Kirkland

In this 1981 celebratory anniversary poster, Robert Rauschenberg honored Lane Kirkland, president of the AFL-CIO from 1979 to 1995, highlighting his portrait in bright orange. In addition to strengthening the influence of the AFL-CIO, Kirkland made the organization's resources available to sustain Poland's Solidarity Movement, thus contributing to the collapse of that nation's Communist regime. Rauschenberg testifies to the longstanding importance of the AFL-CIO and its diverse membership with his juxtaposition of historic and contemporary photographs. Seals from each of the unions represented by the AFL-CIO form the foundation layer of the poster. Rauschenberg demonstrated his admiration for Kirkland, a close friend since the mid-1960s, by presenting him with this first number of the edition and personalizing it with an inscription.

GRACE JONES/NIGHTCLUBBING

NOUVEL ALBUM

ISLAND

"I´VE SEEN THAT FACE BEFORE"
(LIBERTANGO)

c'est une publication
phonogram

Grace Jones/Nightclubbing
Grace Jones | born 1948

Unidentified artist
Color photolithographic halftone poster, c. 1981
81.7 x 53.1 cm (32 3/16 x 20 7/8 in.)
National Portrait Gallery, Smithsonian Institution;
gift of Chisholm Larsson Gallery

Singer-performer Grace Jones firmly established her signature androgynous look with this iconic image advertising her 1981 *Nightclubbing* album and subsequent concerts. With her taut, slim body, gleaming dark skin, square-cut hair, and broad-shouldered masculine jacket with the plunging neckline, Jones satirized gender and racial stereotypes with a fashion-conscious theatricality that became part of her performance. The bold yellow background of the poster sets off the dark, gender-bending silhouette and underscores her sometimes confrontational style. Jones had been a successful model in Paris and then part of Andy Warhol's circle and the disco dance scene of New York. Her cross-dressing, use of the body, and sexualized performance all evoke the complex exploitation and subversion of stereotypes by African American performer Josephine Baker in 1920s Paris. Jones's sleek, trend-setting look echoes the African-inspired geometric stylization of Baker's day, as well as the minimalist aesthetic of her own.

A Tribute to the Music of Thelonious Monk

Thelonious Monk | 1917–1982

Niklaus Troxler (born 1947)
Color silkscreen poster, 1986
128 x 89.8 cm (50 3/8 x 35 3/8 in.)
National Portrait Gallery, Smithsonian Institution

Equal passions for jazz and graphic design motivated artist Niklaus Troxler's innovative posters. Starting in the mid–1970s, he organized an annual music festival in his native Willisau, Switzerland, and his advertising images for those events established his reputation as a graphic artist. "His success is linked to his profound understanding of the work he wants to describe," one admirer has observed. In this poster for a tribute concert to jazz pianist and composer Thelonious Monk, Troxler tried to visualize the composer's favorite composition, "'Round Midnight." Originally trained as a typographer, Troxler ultimately outlined Monk's recognizable, goateed profile with brightly colored lettering. Monk, who transformed jazz with discordant bebop experimentation, was "after new chords, new ways of syncopating, new figurations, new runs." Troxler's unexpected compositions and dazzling color combinations pay tribute to Monk's legacy of improvisation.

A TRIBUTE TO THE MUSIC OF THELONIOUS MONK. Freitag 5. September '86, 20.30 Uhr. Mohren

Jon Hendricks George Adams Bill Hardman

Walter Davis jun. Stafford James and Cliff Barbaro

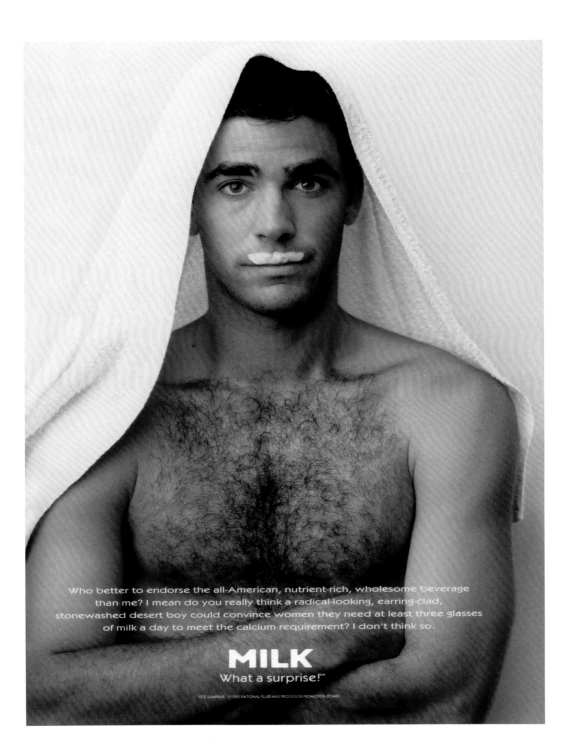

Who better to endorse the all-American, nutrient-rich, wholesome beverage than me? I mean do you really think a radical-looking, earring-clad, stonewashed desert boy could convince women they need at least three glasses of milk a day to meet the calcium requirement? I don't think so.

MILK
What a surprise!™

Milk/What a Surprise!
Pete Sampras | born 1971

Annie Leibovitz (born 1949)
Color photolithographic poster, 1995
80.5 x 59.5 cm (31 11/16 x 23 7/16 in.)
National Portrait Gallery, Smithsonian Institution;
gift of the Chisholm-Larsson Gallery

Tennis star Pete Sampras, the number-one-ranked world champion from 1993 to 1998—and eventual seven-time Wimbledon winner—was a fan of the milk mustache ads and volunteered to be a celebrity subject. The famous campaign was launched in 1995 to boost sales by advertising the health benefits of adults drinking milk. From the beginning, the advertising agency used humor to convey its educational message. The photographs by Annie Leibovitz combined sexy bodies with silly faces and conflated notions of childhood (sloppy milk drinking), adulthood (facial hair), and old age (white mustache). The goofy pictures of popular culture stars proved an instant hit, generating publicity, awards, and parodies. The Sampras poster emphasized his superb physique and quirky habit of tossing a towel over his head between sets. But it says more about 1990s celebrity and its commercial potential than about Sampras's actual prowess on the courts.

Lance

Lance Armstrong | born 1971

Michael Schwab (born 1952)
Color silkscreen poster, 2002
71.1 x 50.8 cm (28 x 20 in.)
National Portrait Gallery, Smithsonian Institution;
gift of Michael Schwab

Cyclist Lance Armstrong began his career
as a brash American with potential, winning
both the CoreStates Race (United States
National Championships) and the World Road
Race Championships in 1993. But after the
1996 Olympics, he was diagnosed with a very
aggressive form of testicular cancer. Overcoming
his illness, he returned to cycling with a renewed
focus, winning a record seven Tour de France
races between 1999 and 2005. In 1997 he had
started the Lance Armstrong Foundation to fight
cancer and raise awareness of the disease. This
2002 silkscreen poster, commemorating his fourth
victory, was commissioned by helmet-maker Giro
Sport Design to raise funds for the foundation
and USA Cycling. Michael Schwab's design
silhouettes Armstrong's black profile against
patriotic stripes and features a yellow helmet, a
color that suggests both the tour leader's jersey
and the foundation's "Livestrong" wristbands.

ARTIST PROOF   8/30   M SCIPIS

Giro

Pirates of the Caribbean
Johnny Depp | born 1963

Unidentified artist
Color photolithographic halftone poster stand-up, 2003
182.9 x 95.4 cm (72 x 37 9/16 in.)
National Portrait Gallery, Smithsonian Institution;
gift of the John Daniel Reaves family

"There was no good reason for this film not to suck," *Rolling Stone* magazine noted about the 2003 movie *Pirates of the Caribbean: The Curse of the Black Pearl,* which was based on a Disney theme park ride. When Johnny Depp agreed to join the cast, his agent called him a lunatic. But Depp, who admired the unfettered looniness of the cartoons he watched with his young daughter, thought he could breathe new life into the pirate cliché. His Captain Jack Sparrow, inspired in part by rocker Keith Richards, was an original and hugely entertaining character. Foppish, outrageous, and fey, festooned with dreadlocks and beaded braids, Depp's pirate helped spawn a blockbuster hit and two sequels. This stand-up poster advertised the shameless zaniness of the movie. implying that Depp's imaginative portrayal, more than the costumes, special effects, and byzantine story, underlies the whole *Pirates* franchise.

Acknowledgments

This book, despite the single authorial voice attached to it, grew out of two processes that are as highly collaborative as a Broadway musical: a museum exhibition and a decades-long effort to collect poster art for the National Portrait Gallery. An exhibition is a theatrical production, with curators, designers, conservators, exhibition staff, research assistants, and educators working together within a compressed period of time to create an experience for our audience. I am greatly indebted to Acting Director Carolyn Carr and all the creative Portrait Gallery staff; they not only lent their talents to this collaborative production, they made it fun. I should single out among them Director of Exhibitions and Collections Management Beverly Cox, who optimistically suggested the idea for this project and remained its staunch advocate; as well as conservator Rosemary Fallon; preparator Ed Myers; and photographer Mark Gulezian.

The much slower process of collecting for an institution, is, I have come to realize, similarly dependent upon others. My own passionate pursuit of poster art was fueled by dealers, collectors, donors, and scholars from other institutions. Within this category, I should thank Jack Rennert, Jack Banning, the Schreyer family, Louis Bixenman, Robert Chisholm, Lars Larsson, Jason Pellecchia, George Theofiles, Mel Meehan, Saul Zalesch, Elena Milley, and Joann Moser. The many gifts credited in these pages attest to the generous enthusiasm of that poster community. The encouragement of my collecting over the years from Directors Alan Fern and Marc Pachter and fellow curators within the Portrait Gallery proved to be of equal importance.

Especially critical for this project were my colleagues Anne Goodyear and Amy Baskette, whose expertise, writing, research, and administrative skills added immeasurably. I am vividly aware of how much of their work is embedded in this volume and hope they understand the depth of my gratitude. Portrait Gallery historians—Sidney Hart, David Ward, Amy Henderson, James Barber, and Fred Voss—all aided our research efforts over time, as did interns, fellows, and assistants, including Beth Isaacson, Lauren Johnson, Libby Miles, Hannah Wong, Kerry Roeder, Breanne Robertson, Charlotte Gaither, LuLen Walker, and Ann Wagner. This book is the culmination of those years of collecting, learning, and thinking about poster art, and all of those voices are represented in its pages.

I am always humbled to think how profoundly the support and wisdom of John Daniel, Paul, and Caroline Reaves underlie any effort of mine. And I will ever be grateful for the talent, taste, perfectionism, and wicked humor of NPG's head of publications, Dru Dowdy. She has been the tireless midwife for many projects of mine, and I owe her endless thanks. I dedicate this book to her.

Wendy Wick Reaves
Curator of Prints and Drawings
National Portrait Gallery, Smithsonian Institution

Notes on Sources

Ballyhoo!: Posters as Portraiture:
"Pictures meant to be seen," in A. Hyatt Mayor, *Prints and People: A Social History of Printed Pictures* (Princeton, N.J.: Princeton University Press, 1980), unpaginated (at illustration 640). "Telegraph utterance," in W. Lewis Fraser, "The Century's American Artists' Series: Sergeant Kendall," *The Century* 50 (July 1895): 478. "I had the conviction," in Walton Rawls, *Wake Up America! World War I and the American Poster* (New York: Abbeville, 1988), 149–50. "To place upon every wall," in ibid., 150. "News, education," in Roland Marchand, *Advertising the American Dream: Making Way for Modernity, 1920–1940* (Berkeley: University of California Press, 1985), 96. "Search for authority," in ibid., 6. "The Big Poster Hang-Up," in "The Great Poster Wave," *Life,* Sept. 1, 1967, cover. "Postermania," in Hilton Kramer, "Postermania," *New York Times Magazine,* Feb. 11, 1968. "Pop Goes the Poster," in Herbert Gold, "Pop Goes the Poster," *Saturday Evening Post,* Mar. 23, 1968, 32. "Son of button," in ibid., 34. "Gobbled up," in "Great Poster Wave," 36. "Wellesley girls," in "The Coolest Things," *Newsweek,* Mar. 6, 1967, 87. "Stylistic complacency," in *The Push Pin Style* (Palo Alto: Communication Arts Magazine, 1970), unpaginated. "All the things," in Milton Glaser, introduction to *The Push Pin Graphic: A Quarter Century of Innovative Design and Illustration* by Seymour Chwast (San Francisco: Chronicle Books, 2004), 8. "Jolt the eye," in "Great Poster Wave," 36. "Psychedelicacies," in ibid., 42. "Overused," in Jay Schulberg, *The Milk Mustache Book* (New York: Ballantine, 1998), xi.

Folies-Bergère La Loïe Fuller: "A hooray of reds," in Alain Weil, *The Poster: A Worldwide Survey and History* (Boston: G. K. Hall, 1985), 27.

Robert Blum's Great Decorative Painting in January Scribner's: "A telegraph utterance," in Fraser, "The Century's American Artists' Series," 478.

Miss Ada Rehan: "Buoyant, scintillant," in Otis Skinner, *Footlights and Spotlights* (New York: Blue Ribbon Books, 1923), 138.

Major Taylor: "Gained all the triumphs," in Marshall W. Taylor, *The Fastest Bicycle Rider in the World* (Worcester, Mass.: Wormley Publishing , c. 1928), x.

Pershing's Crusaders: "Charlie Chaplin and Mary Pickford led," in Larry Wayne Ward, *The Motion Picture Goes to War: The U.S. Government Film Effort during World War I* (Ann Arbor: UMI Research Press, c. 1985), 121.

Djaevlestenen: "Western [film] experiment," in Agnes de Mille, *Dance to the Piper & Promenade Home* (1952; reprint, New York: Da Capo, 1979), 19.

Blixtens Broder: "The wild games," in "Rialto Offers New Bill Hart Feature," *Atlanta Constitution,* Apr. 10, 1921.

Douglas Fairbanks as the Gaucho: "There is, after all," in "Douglas Fairbanks in 'The Gaucho,'" *Christian Science Monitor,* Nov. 29, 1927.

Buster Keaton L'Opérateur: "It seems that the whole universe," in James Agee, "Comedy's Greatest Era," *Life,* Sept. 5, 1949, 82.

Dr. Jekyll/Mr. Hyde: "Expert cunning," in Mordaunt Hall, "Fredric March in a Splendidly Produced Pictorial Version of 'Dr. Jekyll and Mr. Hyde,'" *New York Times,* Jan. 2, 1932. "We are treating Hyde," in "Freud Joins Jekyll-Hyde," *Los Angeles Times*, Sept. 27, 1931.

Greta Garbo in Königin Christine: "Breathtaking and mystical," in Peter B. Flint, "Greta Garbo, 84, Screen Icon Who Fled Her Stardom, Dies," *New York Times,* Apr. 16, 1990.

Yankee Doodle Dandy: "Every time I see him work," in Peter B. Flint, "James Cagney is Dead at 86," *New York Times,* Mar. 31, 1986.

Pvt. Joe Louis Says—"His huge picture" and "exceptionally meritorious service," in Steven Anzovin and Alan Crawford, "Joe Louis Boxer," *The Annual Obituary 1981* (New York: St. Martin's, 1982), 270.

Trinidad: "I must suggest," in Maurice Horn, ed., *The World Encyclopedia of Cartoons* (Detroit: Gale Research, 1980), 98.

Fronte del Porto: "Strode through," in Rick Lyman, "Marlon Brando, Oscar-Winning Actor, is Dead at 80," *New York Times,* July 2, 2004.

Goldwater for President: "Extremism in the defense," in Theodore H. White, *The Making of the President 1964* (New York: Atheneum, 1965), 217.

Count Basie and Band/Stan Getz and Quartet: "Polish was the keynote," in "Concert is Given by Basie and Getz," *New York Times,* Nov. 28, 1963. "Orthodox modernism," in Glaser, introduction to Chwast, *Push Pin Graphic,* 8.

Junior Wells: "Load up the surface," in *San Francisco Rock Poster Art* (San Francisco: San Francisco Museum of Modern Art, 1976), 10.

Butterfield Blues Band: "Probably the most influential," in Peter Selz, "The Hippie Poster," *Graphis* (January 1968),

70. "Playing with foreground and background," in Paul D. Grushkin, *The Art of Rock: Posters from Presley to Punk* (New York: Abbeville, 1987), 72. "Oozes and ebbs," in ibid., 73.

Jefferson Airplane: "Posters in every dimension and description," in "Great Poster Wave," 36.

What becomes a Legend most? (Bette Davis): "Ten cigarettes later," in Peter Rogers, *The Blackglama Story by Peter Rogers* (New York: Simon and Schuster, 1979), 16.

What becomes a Legend most? (Judy Garland): "Somehow it seemed to capture," in Rogers, *Blackglama Story,* 22.

I don't know what will happen now: "As famed in his own medium of protest," in *Time,* March 19, 1945, 21.

Bette Midler: "She's 5'1"," in Rex Reed, "Star-bent Bette: From Tubs to the Top," *Chicago Tribune,* Feb. 20, 1972.

Dog Day Afternoon: "Made me believe," in Gene Siskel, "A (Dog) Day in the Life of the Hostage Taker," *Chicago Tribune,* Oct. 24, 1975.

Apocalypse Now: "Is not another helicopter battle," in Tony Chiu, "Francis Coppola's Cinematic 'Apocalypse' Is Finally at Hand," *New York Times,* Aug. 12, 1979.

A Tribute to the Music of Thelonious Monk: "His success is linked," in *Jazz Blvd.: Niklaus Troxler Posters* (Baden, Switzerland: Lars Müller, 1999), 82. "After new chords," in John S. Wilson, "Thelonious Monk, Created Wry Jazz Melodies and New Harmonies," *New York Times,* Feb. 18, 1982.

Pirates of the Caribbean: "There was no good reason," in Mark Binelli, "The Last Buccaneer," *Rolling Stone,* July 13, 2006, 50.

For Further Reading

Barnicoat, John. *A Concise History of Posters: 1870–1970.* New York: Harry N. Abrams, 1972.

Bird, William L., Jr., and Harry R. Rubenstein. *Design for Victory: World War II Posters on the American Home Front.* New York: Princeton Architectural Press, 1998.

Chwast, Seymour. *The Push Pin Graphic: A Quarter Century of Innovative Design and Illustration.* San Francisco: Chronicle Books, 2004.

Fern, Alan. *Word and Image.* New York: Museum of Modern Art, 1968.

Friedman, Mildred, and Phil Freshman, eds. *Graphic Design in America: A Visual Language History.* Minneapolis: Walker Art Center; New York: Harry Abrams, 1989.

Gold, Herbert. "Pop Goes the Poster." *Saturday Evening Post*, March 23, 1968, 32–35.

"The Great Poster Wave: Expendable Graphic Art Becomes America's Biggest Hang-Up." *Life,* September 1, 1967, 36–43.

Grushkin, Paul D. *The Art of Rock: Posters from Presley to Punk.* New York: Abbeville, 1987.

Harris, Neil. "American Poster Collecting: A Fitful History." *American Art* 12 (Spring 1998): 10–39.

Heyman, Therese. *Posters American Style.* New York: Harry N. Abrams, 1998.

Hutchison, Harold F. *The Poster: An Illustrated History from 1860.* New York: Viking, [1968].

Kiehl, David W. *American Art Posters of the 1890s.* New York: Harry N. Abrams, 1987.

Marchand, Roland. *Advertising the American Dream: Making Way for Modernity, 1920–1940.* Berkeley: University of California Press, 1985.

Rawls, Walton. *Wake Up America! World War I and the American Poster.* New York: Abbeville, 1988.

Rennert, Jack. *100 Years of Circus Posters.* New York: Avon Books, 1974.

Weil, Alain. *The Poster: A Worldwide Survey and History.* Boston: G. K. Hall, 1985.

Wrede, Stuart. *The Modern Poster.* New York: Museum of Modern Art, 1988.

Index

Copyrights